> "We may live without poetry, music and art;
> We may live without conscience, and live without heart;
> We may live without friends, we may live without books;
> But civilized man cannot live without cooks".
>
> Owen Meredith 1831-1891

Let's cook!

Best wishes,

Philip Johnson's

more recipes from an Australian bistro

e'cco 2

RANDOM HOUSE AUSTRALIA

acknowledgements

It's often said that to run a successful business, you must first surround yourself with the right people.

My people, who deserve all my thanks and grateful acknowledgements, are:

Linda Franz and Bevan Smith, and the entire – and untiring – kitchen brigade.

Ian White and Tracey Rayner, my floor managers, and their brilliant team.

Carol Weeks, whose skills turned many a scribbled recipe into a legible one.

Tony Waller, who definitively captures the spirit of e'cco and its food on film.

Random House Australia, who believed in me from the beginning.

And especially to Shirley, who takes care of everything else in our lives, allowing me to get on with doing what I love.

Published in Australia by Random House Australia Pty. Ltd.
20 Alfred Street, Milsons Point, NSW Australia 2061
Fax: 61 2 9955 3381
http://www.randomhouse.com.au

Sydney New York Toronto London Auckland Johannesburg
and agencies throughout the world

First published in 2002
Copyright © Philip Johnson (Recipes) 2002

National Library of Australia
Cataloguing-in-Publication Data

Johnson, Philip, 1959
e'cco 2

Includes index
ISBN 1 74051 114 X

1. Cookery, Australian. I. e'cco (Restaurant). II. Title.

641.5994

Design: Anne Marie Cummins, Justin Thomas for amcdesign
Editor: Lucy Tumanow-West
Publisher: James Mills-Hicks
Production Manager: Angela Alegounarias
Publishing Co-ordinator: Anabel Pandiella

Film separation by Response Colour Graphics Pty. Ltd
Printed by Tien Wah Press (PTE) Limited in Singapore

Photographs were reproduced with the kind permission of:
Tony Waller (cover and internal photographs);
Brendan Read (photograph of Philip Johnson, photograph of smoked quail with witlof, parsnip, pear & honey)

Right: Vanilla friands, blueberries & Amaretto cream (recipe page 143)

Philip Johnson's

more recipes from an Australian bistro

écco 2

contents

Introduction 8
Starters 11

contents

Desserts 99

Basics 153

introduction

Something happened to me during the time I was writing this book that really brought home to me why I love writing about food, talking about food and, every day of my life, cooking and eating food.

I was in New Zealand appearing at their very first Masterclass. Food and wine presenters had gathered from around the world to give classes in their specialty fields.

When I was growing up near Christchurch, Alison Holst was the shining star of the nation's food scene. Having written a staggering 80 cookbooks to date and with sales close to 4 million – not bad for a country with a population of just 3.5 million – she is to New Zealanders what Margaret Fulton and Stephanie Alexander are to Australians, Julia Child to the Americans, or Elizabeth David and Delia Smith are to the British.

After my first class, Alison came up to me with her sister Claire Ferguson, also an extremely successful author and food stylist in London, and told me it was one of the very best classes she had ever seen.

It's always satisfying to be acknowledged by your peers. But this was Alison Holst, someone whose books had sat on my mother's kitchen shelf when I was a child. (Along with the collection of recipes from the local kindergarten mums – I still love those and they really do work.)

Apart from making me proud, it proved to me all over again that putting your head down, believing in yourself and working hard might not be the only way to get where you want to go. But it certainly has its rewards.

I've long harboured the thought that for a chef to cook well, they should probably cook what they like to eat. Starters and desserts is the way I like to eat, and quite often when I'm eating with my wife Shirley, we will share several starters between us.

So, not surprisingly, this book is just that; a collection of starters and desserts from the menus at e'cco.

I've noticed in the restaurant that for a lot of people starters and desserts are a chance to experiment, to try something a little different that perhaps they've never considered having before. Just as often we'll hear customers say to each other 'Let's have two entrées, because I really, really want to have dessert.' I've even known people to do it the other way around: one starter and two desserts.

My kind of people.

From a cook's point of view, because starters and desserts can be slightly unpredictable, they're much more fun and liberating, too, because it's a lot easier to be creative and adventurous with your flavours and combinations in a starter or dessert. When you're devising a recipe for a main dish, you have to take into account all the components that people traditionally expect: a serve of protein, a vegetable, a starch such as potato, pasta, rice, etc.

With starters and desserts, you're let off the leash a bit.

Because a starter or dessert is smaller than a main dish, it can also have an enhanced visual appeal. One of those rare occasions when less really is more. And with starters and desserts, you can enjoy the freedom to experiment a little, but I also believe you've got to be just as disciplined in your approach to quality as you would be with your main course. Paring back brings its own challenges, in food as in life, in the home cook's kitchen as much as in a restaurant. When there's nowhere to hide, you really want to be sure you're working with the very best ingredients you can find.

Truth in dining, you could call it.

But on the upside – I'm an optimist, even in the busiest kitchen I can always find an upside – the better the produce, the less you have to do to it.

People have said to me that the dessert list at e'cco is a surprise after the fresh and simple flavours of the savoury dishes. Sweet. Tart. Exotic. You'll find all those elements here. The starters, too, use familiar and delicious ingredients in unexpected ways to achieve the most rewarding results.

What both the starters and desserts have in common is consistently good-quality ingredients integrating together to create simple, perfectly matched flavours. These are recipes that are accessible, fresh, and you can cook and enjoy them often.

My first book, *Philip Johnson's e'cco - recipes from an Australian bistro,* went a long way to proving that restaurant food can be transformed for the home environment. Thinking about, tasting and testing the recipes for this book, although not exactly easy, has again been very rewarding. I found, after the first book, that it's a bit like the restaurant industry: addictive.

Just like the first book, I'd like this new one to be used as a guide, to inspire you to make the most of locally produced seasonal foods. We're not reinventing the wheel. This is food, nothing more. But equally, it's nothing less.

I recently received an email and this quote was attached: "I don't suffer from insanity – I enjoy every minute of it." I think it really sums up our hectic existence. And I do believe that to totally succeed in life, you must be doing what you love most, whatever that may be.

Fulfilment, most of us find, usually comes as a by-product of this.

Philip Johnson

starters

Atlantic salmon, hokkien noodles, pak choy, Asian mushrooms, chilli, ginger & lime

Serves 6

Fresh hokkien noodles are readily available in Chinatown. The kaffir lime leaves are best either fresh or frozen rather than dried.

6 x 120g (720g/1½ lb total) portions Atlantic salmon, skin on, scaled and pin-boned

salt/freshly ground black pepper

olive oil

300g (10½ oz) hokkien noodles

150g (5 oz) button mushrooms, sliced

150g (5 oz) shiitake mushrooms, sliced

100g (3½ oz) enoki mushrooms

300g (10½ oz) pak choy

1 cup picked coriander leaves

Stock infusion

1 litre (1¾ pints) chicken stock (Basics page 158)

3 star anise

3 red chillies, seeds removed and chopped

3 cloves garlic, sliced

100g (3½ oz) fresh ginger, peeled and sliced

2 sticks lemongrass, smashed

3 kaffir lime leaves, shredded

Chilli and mustard seed dressing

2 tablespoons (40ml/1½ fl oz) peanut oil

2 tablespoons black or brown mustard seeds

2 cloves garlic, thinly sliced

⅓ cup red chillies, sliced diagonally

⅓ cup fresh ginger, peeled and julienned

½ cup (125g/4½ oz) palm sugar

2 teaspoons (10ml) fish sauce

juice of 6 limes

To make stock infusion, in a medium saucepan simmer chicken stock until reduced by half. Add star anise, chillies, garlic and ginger. Continue to simmer for 15 minutes, then remove from heat. Add lemongrass and kaffir lime leaves and leave to infuse for a further 30 minutes. Strain, return stock to pan and set aside.

To make dressing, heat oil in a small saucepan until very hot. Add mustard seeds and cook for 2–3 minutes – they will begin to pop. Add garlic and cook until golden and beginning to crisp. Next add chillies, then ginger, and cook for a further 2 minutes. Remove from heat and add palm sugar, fish sauce and lime juice to taste. Set aside.

Season salmon skin with salt and pepper. Heat a heavy-based or non-stick frying pan over high heat and add a little olive oil. Sear salmon, skin-side down, until a good colour is achieved. Reduce heat to moderate, turn salmon and cook for a further 3–5 minutes or until medium rare.

Meanwhile, bring infused stock to the boil, add hokkien noodles and cook briefly. Drain noodles, reserving stock.

In a separate pan, sauté mushrooms in a little hot oil until almost cooked. Add pak choy and season to taste. Cook until pak choy just begins to soften.

To serve, divide pak choy and mushrooms between shallow bowls and place noodles on top. Pour a small amount of stock over, then coriander leaves. Place salmon on top, skin-side up. Stir dressing well and generously spoon over salmon.

Baked goat's cheese tart with salad of rocket & pear

Serves 9

There are so many high-quality goat's cheeses on the Australian market, there is little need to use the imported varieties. We use either Camille Mortaud's cheese from Gympie in Queensland, Charles Parsons' from Charella Goat Dairy in Mudgeeraba on the Gold Coast Hinterland, Gabrielle Kervella's from Western Australia or one from Milawa in northeast Victoria. The three most common varieties of goat's cheese are blanc (white), rolled in ash, and aged, which has an outer mould similar to camembert. For this tart, it is better to use the blanc.

1 savoury shortcrust pastry shell (Basics page 154)

Filling

600ml (1 pint) pouring cream (35% butterfat)

6 eggs

2 teaspoons freshly chopped thyme leaves

salt/freshly ground black pepper

300g (10½ oz) soft fresh goat's cheese, broken into tablespoon-sized chunks

Salad

3 ripe but firm pears, sliced

150g (5 oz) rocket, washed

3–4 red radishes, sliced finely

lemon dressing (Basics page 160)

salt/freshly ground black pepper

Prepare pastry as recipe directs and blind bake (Basics page 155).

Preheat oven to 130°C (265°F).

To make the filling, whisk cream, eggs and thyme together and season to taste.

Place goat's cheese in base of cooled tart shell. Carefully pour filling over cheese.

Bake 40–50 minutes or until filling is just set. Cool slightly before cutting into 9 portions.

To make salad, in a large bowl combine pears, rocket and radishes. Coat with enough lemon dressing to moisten leaves. Season to taste.

To serve, place a wedge of warm tart in the centre of each plate and arrange a portion of salad alongside.

Baked parmesan & thyme tart with red onion jam

Serves 9

1 savoury shortcrust pastry shell (Basics page 154)

red onion jam (Basics page 166)

bitter greens, such as radicchio, witlof,
    rocket and watercress

red wine vinaigrette (Basics page 161)

shaved parmesan

Filling

1 onion, cut into fine dice

600ml (1 pint) pouring cream (35% butterfat)

6 eggs

140g (5 oz) parmesan, grated

2 teaspoons freshly chopped thyme leaves

salt/freshly ground black pepper

Prepare shortcrust pastry shell and bake blind (Basics page 155) as recipe directs.

Prepare red onion jam as recipe directs.

Preheat oven to 130°C (265°F).

To make filling, sauté onion until soft but without colour. Whisk together cream, eggs, parmesan, thyme and onion. Season well.

Carefully pour mixture into prepared pastry shell and bake for 40 minutes or until filling is just set.

Combine greens and dress with enough vinaigrette to moisten.

To serve, place a wedge of warm tart in the centre of each plate and arrange a portion of salad to one side. Place slices of shaved parmesan against each tart. Serve with a generous spoonful of warmed red onion jam.

Blue eye cod, saffron potatoes, baby leeks, tomato, mint & orange salsa

Serves 6

We have specified blue eye cod but this can be substituted with your favourite white fish.

6 x 120g (720g/1½ lb total) blue eye cod fillets, skinless, boneless

½ cup (125g/4½ oz) plain flour

½ cup (125ml/4½ fl oz) clarified butter, melted (Basics page 155)

500ml (18 fl oz) chicken stock (Basics page 158)

2 tablespoons (40g/1½ oz) unsalted butter

good pinch saffron

12 medium southern gold (pink-eye) potatoes, steamed and peeled

1 bunch baby leeks, trimmed and washed, sliced diagonally into rings

knob of unsalted butter

Tomato mint & orange salsa

6 roma tomatoes

1 small red onion, diced

pinch dried chilli

zest of 1 orange

juice of 2 oranges

extra-virgin olive oil

salt/freshly ground black pepper

¼ cup mint, picked and washed

To make salsa, cut tomatoes into quarters, discard seeds and finely dice. Combine in bowl with onion, dried chilli, orange zest and juice, a splash of olive oil, salt and pepper. Cover and allow to infuse for 30 minutes.

Preheat grill to hot. Coat fish with flour and shake off excess. Place fish on greased oven tray, brush with clarified butter and season with salt and pepper. Grill fish until just cooked and golden, approximately 8 minutes.

Meanwhile, place chicken stock, butter and saffron into a large pot and bring to the boil. Boil for several minutes to allow saffron to infuse. Cut potatoes in half. Reduce heat and place potatoes in saffron stock. Allow to heat through.

Pour off some of the stock, being careful not to break the potatoes. In a clean pan, reduce this stock to a sauce consistency.

In a non-stick or heavy-based pan, sauté leeks with unsalted butter until softened (no colour).

To serve, using a slotted spoon, place 3–4 potato halves in the centre of each plate. Place leeks on top of potatoes. Rest fish on top of leeks and drizzle saffron sauce over potatoes and around edge of plate. Lastly, fold mint into salsa and generously spoon over fish.

Braised rabbit, wet polenta & leeks

Serves 6

If you cannot buy rabbit legs on their own, you may need to buy a whole rabbit, which will usually weigh between 1.2kg (2½ lb) and 1.6kg (3 lb). Ask the butcher to remove the hind legs for this recipe, or you may have to do it yourself. The loins can be removed from the carcass and simply grilled to use in a warm salad. The remaining carcass and front legs are best used for stock or soup.

¼ cup (60ml/2 fl oz) extra-virgin olive oil

3 cloves garlic, finely crushed

1 tablespoon fresh thyme, chopped

2 bay leaves

6 rabbit legs (hindquarter)

wet polenta (Basics page 167)

12 baby leeks

salt/freshly ground black pepper

grated parmesan

jus (Basics page 159)

seeded mustard

Combine oil, garlic, thyme and bay leaves. Pour over rabbit legs in a glass or ceramic dish. Cover and marinate overnight in the refrigerator.

Prepare wet polenta as recipe directs.

Trim green ends from leeks. Slice each leek into 6–8cm (2–3 in) lengths. Blanch in boiling salted water until tender, then refresh in cold water. Drain.

Preheat oven to 180°C (350°F).

Remove rabbit legs from marinade and season. Heat a heavy, ovenproof pan over moderate heat. Sear rabbit legs, turning regularly, until good colour is achieved.

Place pan in oven and cook for approximately 20 minutes or until rabbit is just cooked. Transfer rabbit and cooking juices to a plate and cover loosely with aluminium foil. Rest for at least 10 minutes.

Place blanched leeks into the same pan, warm through in oven until some colour is achieved, approximately 5–8 minutes.

To serve, heat polenta and place a spoonful on each plate, just off-centre. Rest a rabbit leg beside polenta with leeks alongside. Place a little parmesan on top of polenta. Heat jus with enough seeded mustard to taste. Pour over rabbit.

Buffalo mozzarella with caponata & garlic bruschetta

Serves 6

For many years we have had to be content with cow's milk mozzarella, but with Australia's burgeoning cheese industry, fresh, traditionally made buffalo milk mozzarella is now available from Gippsland in Victoria. However, if you can obtain the imported fresh Italian buffalo mozzarella, I believe the flavour to be far superior.

6 slices ciabatta (or similar crusty Italian bread)

garlic confit (Basics page 168)

caponata (Basics page 168), warm or at room temperature

500g (1 lb) buffalo mozzarella

extra-virgin olive oil

freshly ground black pepper

Toast ciabatta and spread liberally with garlic confit.

Place a generous spoonful of caponata on each plate.

Place several slices of mozzarella beside caponata. Place garlic bruschetta next to mozzarella. Drizzle with oil and finish with a good grinding of black pepper.

Chicken fillets with saffron couscous, almonds, currants & wilted spinach

Serves 6

600g (1¼ lb) chicken tenderloin fillets, trimmed

150g (5 oz) English spinach, stems removed

extra-virgin olive oil

1 cup (250ml/9 fl oz) Greek-style yoghurt

Marinade

2 cloves garlic, crushed

1 teaspoon fresh thyme leaves, chopped

pinch dried chilli

¼ cup (60ml/2 fl oz) extra-virgin olive oil

Saffron couscous

2 cups (500ml/18 fl oz) chicken stock
  (Basics page 158)

125g (4½ oz) unsalted butter

pinch saffron

2 cups (500g/1 lb) couscous

salt/freshly ground black pepper

½ cup (125g/4½ oz) currants, moistened with a little
  red wine vinegar and left to infuse overnight

½ cup (125g/4½ oz) whole blanched almonds,
  toasted and roughly chopped

dash of extra-virgin olive oil

1 cup coriander sprigs, washed and spun

Combine all marinade ingredients in a large bowl. Marinate chicken fillets for several hours or overnight.

To make couscous, bring chicken stock, butter, saffron and seasoning to the boil in a saucepan.

Place couscous into a large bowl, then pour boiling stock over. Stir briefly with a fork to ensure all grains are covered.

Cover the bowl with plastic wrap and set aside to steam for 20 minutes. Once cooled to room temperature, toss with currants, almonds, olive oil and coriander. Adjust seasoning.

Remove chicken from marinade and cook in a heavy-based frying pan over high heat, turning once. Remove from pan.

Wilt spinach in a hot pan with a little olive oil, salt and pepper.

To serve, place a large spoonful of couscous in the centre of each plate. Top with 2–3 chicken fillets. Place spinach on top of chicken. Top with a spoonful of yoghurt.

Chicken tenderloin with baked sweet potato, chorizo, coriander & chilli jam

Serves 6

If Spanish-style chorizo sausage is unavailable, a similar spicy Italian sausage would work well. You would probably have to cook it whole and then slice it, as it is unlikely Italian sausage could be sliced as a cured chorizo can.

18 chicken tenderloin fillets, cleaned and trimmed if necessary

3 sweet potatoes (kumera)

olive oil

salt/freshly ground black pepper

2 chorizo sausages, sliced diagonally

12 stems broccolini (or broccoli)

1/2 cup coriander leaves, picked and washed

chilli jam/chilli tomato chutney (Basics page 157)

jus (Basics page 159)

Marinade

1/4 cup (60ml/2 fl oz) extra-virgin olive oil

pinch chilli flakes

juice and grated zest of half a lemon

heaped teaspoon thyme leaves, freshly chopped

Combine all the marinade ingredients. Place tenderloins in a large bowl or dish and coat with marinade. Refrigerate overnight.

Make chilli jam as recipe directs.

Preheat oven to 180°C (350°F). Peel sweet potatoes and slice into discs approximately 1cm (1/2 in) thick. Lay sweet potatoes on non-stick tray or baking tray lined with non-stick baking (silicone) paper. Brush sweet potato with olive oil, season and bake for 20 minutes or until tender.

When ready to prepare meal, bring a saucepan of salted water to the boil (for broccolini).

Return sweet potato to oven to reheat if necessary.

Remove chicken tenderloins from marinade and drain off excess oil. Heat a non-stick frying pan over high heat and cook tenderloins (you will probably need to do this in 2 or 3 batches). Set aside and keep warm.

In the same pan, quickly sauté the chorizo slices and drain on kitchen paper.

Place broccolini in boiling water for several minutes.

To serve, place 2 slices sweet potato in centre of each plate. Top with chorizo, coriander and a generous spoonful of chilli jam. Rest 2 broccolini pieces alongside. Arrange 3 chicken tenderloins on top. Drizzle a little jus over and around chicken if desired.

Coral trout, fennel & blood orange salad with almond aioli

Serves 6

Coral trout may be substituted for a similar white-fleshed fish.

If blood oranges are out of season, the recipe works equally well with seedless oranges.

6 x 120g (750g/1½ lb total) coral trout portions, skin on, scaled and pin-boned

½ cup (125ml/4½ fl oz) clarified butter (Basics page 155), melted

salt/freshly ground black pepper

burnt orange vinaigrette (Basics page 162)

6 lemon wedges, to serve

Almond aioli

1 cup (250ml/9 fl oz) roasted garlic mayonnaise (Basics page 156)

½ cup (125g/4½ oz) almonds, roasted in moderate oven until golden brown, cooled and chopped

Salad

2 large or 3 small fennel bulbs, outer leaves and core discarded, finely sliced/shaved

3 Jerusalem artichokes, peeled and shaved

4 blood oranges, peeled and sliced into 5 rounds each

½ red onion, finely sliced lengthwise

1 cup flat-leaf parsley, picked

¼ cup finely chopped chives

salt/freshly ground black pepper

To make almond aioli, first prepare roasted garlic mayonnaise as recipe directs. Transfer mayonnaise into a bowl and fold through almonds. Thin with a little hot water to dropping consistency. Reserve remaining mayonnaise for another use.

To cook trout, preheat grill to high. Place skin-side up on a greased oven tray and brush skin with clarified butter. Season, then grill fish for approximately 8 minutes, or until cooked but still moist.

While fish is cooking, prepare vinaigrette as recipe directs. Place salad ingredients into a bowl. Dress with enough vinaigrette to moisten.

To serve, divide salad evenly between 6 plates, spooning any excess dressing over. Place a piece of fish, skin-side up, on top of salad, finishing with a generous spoonful of almond aioli and a wedge of lemon.

Right: Coral trout, fennel & blood orange salad with almond aioli

Left: Atlantic salmon, hokkien noodles, pak choy, Asian mushrooms, chilli, ginger & lime (recipe page 12)

Right: Buffalo mozzarella with caponata & garlic bruschetta (recipe page 17)

Left: Chicken tenderloin with baked sweet potato, chorizo, coriander & chilli jam (recipe page 19)

Right: Eye fillet, garlic & herb mash, caramelised red onion & wild mushrooms (recipe page 31)

Left: Fried whiting with watercress
& red pepper salsa
(recipe page 33)

Right: Hervey Bay scallops,
cos leaves, apple, cashews &
curry vinaigrette
(recipe page 79)

Cracked pepper tartlet, sautéed duck livers, shallots & port

Serves 6

The pepper in the pastry works well with this dish and gives it great sharpness. If you don't like that much pepper, either cut down the quantity or try adding some fresh herbs to the pastry as an alternative.

1 quantity savoury shortcrust pastry (Basics page 154)

2 tablespoons kibbled pepper

10 shallots, sliced

2 cloves garlic, chopped

olive oil

1 cup (250ml/9 fl oz) good-quality port

½ cup (125ml/4½ fl oz) good-quality red wine

400ml (14 fl oz) jus (Basics page 159)

salt/freshly ground black pepper

olive oil

1.2kg (2½ lb) duck livers, cleaned and trimmed

chicken stock (Basics page 158)

¼ cup chopped green (spring) onions

12 slices pancetta, grilled until crisp

Prepare pastry as recipe directs, incorporating kibbled pepper into mixture with flour.

Roll out and line six 8cm (3 in) tart cases (preferably with removable bases).

Blind bake, pricking pastry rather than using weights (Basics page 155). Fully cook pastry cases and set aside to cool.

To cook duck livers, sauté shallots and garlic in oil until shallots are golden.

Deglaze the pan with port and red wine. Reduce until the pan is almost dry. Add jus and return to the boil. Season to taste and set aside.

Heat a large heavy-based pan over high heat. Add a little oil to the pan and quickly seal duck livers. Add sauce, thinning with a little chicken stock if necessary.

Simmer briefly until livers are cooked to medium, then stir in green onions.

To serve, divide duck livers between warmed pastry cases. Top each with two slices of crisp pancetta.

Left: Cracked pepper tartlet, sautéed duck livers, shallots & port

Egg fettuccine with chorizo, roasted peppers & artichokes

Serves 6

If you can buy the Italian marinated artichokes with stems attached, they look much better visually than the artichoke hearts.

red pepper essence (Basics page 164)

500g (1 lb) egg fettuccine

4 fresh chorizo sausages, cut diagonally into 1cm (1/2 in) thick slices

1 onion, diced

2 cloves garlic, crushed

2 red and 1 yellow pepper (capsicum), roasted, peeled, seeded and sliced (Basics page 164)

6 bottled artichokes, quartered

1 cup basil leaves

salt/freshly ground black pepper

shaved parmesan

Prepare red pepper essence as recipe directs.

Cook fettuccine in boiling salted water until al dente.

Meanwhile, sauté sausages over high heat until coloured. Remove from pan and discard excess fat. Sweat onion and garlic in the same pan. Add peppers (capsicum) and artichokes. Return sausages to pan. Stir through drained fettuccine and add basil leaves. Season to taste.

To serve, spoon into deep bowls and top with shaved parmesan.

Eye fillet, garlic & herb mash, caramelised red onion & wild mushrooms

Serves 6

There was a time when we were starved for a variety of mushrooms, but good greengrocers now carry a wide range. A couple of varieties we haven't mentioned are slippery jacks and pine mushrooms, which are grown in Victoria and would be fantastic in this dish (but are seasonal).

6 x 120g (720g/1¹/₂ lb total) eye fillets of beef, centre cut

olive oil

salt/freshly ground black pepper

knob of unsalted butter

1 teaspoon fresh thyme, chopped

1 clove garlic, crushed

300g (10¹/₂ oz) assorted mushrooms (such as swiss browns, wood ear, enoki, shiitake, oyster), torn or sliced to a similar size

salt/freshly ground black pepper

jus (Basics page 159)

red onion jam, warmed (Basics page 166)

Garlic & herb mash

1.2kg (2¹/₂ lb) pink-skinned waxy potatoes such as desiree, peeled and diced

250ml (9 fl oz) milk

125ml (4¹/₂ fl oz) pouring cream (35% butterfat)

125g (4¹/₂ oz) unsalted butter

1 head garlic confit (Basics page 168)

¹/₂ cup green (spring) onions, thinly sliced diagonally

2 tablespoons flat-leaf parsley, chopped

2 tablespoons chives, chopped

salt/freshly ground white pepper

To make mash, boil potatoes in salted water until tender. Drain, then pass through a mouli or mash. Place milk, cream and butter in a saucepan, bring to the boil, then gradually stir into potatoes to achieve a light, smooth consistency. Squeeze flesh from garlic confit into mash and mix well. Fold in green onions, parsley and chives. Season with salt and white pepper.

To cook the steak, heat a wide, heavy-based frying pan over very high heat. Brush steaks with olive oil and season both sides with salt and pepper. Sear steaks on one side until good colour is achieved, turn, reduce heat slightly and cook until pink (medium). Remove from pan and set aside to rest.

Using the same pan, pour off any excess fat and add butter, thyme, garlic, mushrooms, salt and pepper. Cook until mushrooms have softened.

To serve, place a spoonful of garlic and herb mash into the centre of each plate. Top with eye fillet and drizzle with jus. Arrange mushrooms on top of steak. Serve red onion jam to one side.

Fremantle sardines with new potatoes, saffron & blood oranges

Serves 6

Fremantle in Western Australia has for years had brilliant sardines, available fresh or marinated. Although we've used marinated sardines in this recipe, it would work equally well with grilled sardine fillets or perhaps pan-fried garfish.

If blood oranges are out of season, substitute with seedless oranges.

18 baby new potatoes, skin intact

75g (3 oz) frisèe, washed and spun

75g (3 oz) watercress, washed and spun

24 marinated sardines, preferably from Fremantle

freshly ground black pepper

Dressing

zest of 3 blood oranges

juice of 5 blood oranges

1 cup (250ml/9 fl oz) extra-virgin olive oil

6 blood oranges, peeled and segmented

1 chilli, seeds removed, finely diced

¼ cup flat-leaf parsley leaves, washed and sliced

pinch saffron, dry roasted

salt/freshly ground black pepper

To make dressing, in a large bowl, whisk together orange zest, juice and oil. Stir in orange segments, chilli, parsley and saffron and check seasoning.

Steam potatoes over boiling water until tender. While still hot, slice in half and place in dressing to absorb flavours. Allow to cool to room temperature.

Combine frisèe and watercress.

To serve, divide dressed potatoes and orange segments between the plates. Place 2 sardines on top of potatoes. Arrange frisèe and watercress on top of sardines and drizzle liberally with dressing. Place remaining sardines on top of greens. Finish with a good grinding of black pepper.

Fried whiting with watercress & red pepper salsa

Serves 6

1 cup (250g/9 oz) self-raising flour
1/4 cup (60g/2 oz) cornflour
375ml (13 fl oz) full strength malt beer
salt/freshly ground black pepper
6 x 120g whiting fillets (720g/1 1/2 lb total)
plain flour
oil for deep frying
300g (10 1/2 oz) watercress, well washed
6 lime halves

Salsa

2 red and 2 yellow peppers (capsicum), roasted,
  peeled and diced (Basics page 164)
2 gourmet tomatoes, seeded and diced
1 red onion, diced
1 chilli, seeded and sliced
1/4 cup salted capers, well rinsed
salt/freshly ground black pepper
red wine vinaigrette (Basics page 161)

Place self-raising flour and cornflour into a bowl and make a well in the centre. Gradually mix in beer, taking care not to overwork batter. Season and set aside to rest for at least 30 minutes. This will enable any small lumps in batter to dissipate.

Dust whiting fillets in plain flour then dip into batter, draining off excess.

Gently heat oil to 180°C (350°F) in a deep fryer or wok. Fry fillets in small batches until batter is crisp and golden. Drain on absorbent paper.

To make the salsa, lightly mix together peppers, tomatoes, onion, chilli and capers. Season to taste and moisten with red wine vinaigrette.

To serve, divide watercress between plates and top with salsa. Place whiting fillets alongside and finish with half a lime.

Grilled quail, wild rocket, mustard fruits & pancetta

Serves 6

Wild rocket usually has a larger leaf and more pronounced peppery flavour than the hydroponic varieties.

We use quails from Rannoch Farm in Tasmania and have done so for over 10 years because they have consistently been of exceptional quality. The quails come butterflied in packs of 6 and only need the thigh bone removed.

1 cup (250ml/9 fl oz) mayonnaise (Basics page 156)

1 tablespoon (20ml) seeded mustard

2 tablespoons chives, chopped

6 quail, deboned and butterflied

olive oil

salt/freshly ground black pepper

1 cup (250g/9 oz) assorted mustard fruits (Glossary) in syrup, sliced

150g (5 oz) wild rocket, washed and spun

1 small red onion, cut into fine rings

12 slices pancetta, grilled until crisp

jus (Basics page 159), optional

Combine mayonnaise, mustard and chives. Set aside.

Heat a large ridged grill or heavy-based pan over high heat. Brush quail with olive oil and season. Place skin-side down on grill or hot pan to sear until good colour is achieved. Turn quail and continue to cook until pink (medium). Remove from pan and allow to rest briefly. Divide each quail into 2 halves.

To serve, place mustard fruits with syrup in a circle on each plate, to three quarters of the plate's diameter. Toss rocket with mustard mayonnaise and onion rings. Arrange in centre of plate. Place 2 quail halves on top of rocket. Finish with grilled pancetta and drizzle with a little hot jus.

Grilled quail, zucchini, pine nuts, sherry-soaked raisins & basil

Serves 6

This is a very simple dish but quality ingredients are paramount. Use the best-quality butter and a good Spanish sherry. These two items alone make a huge difference to the dish.

The sherry we use is Pedro Ximenez by Valdespino, from Jerez in Spain, which has a sweet raisin flavour. Probably the best butter you can buy is the French brand Lescure, available in good deli's, but expensive. A good Australian butter is Kirk's from Victoria.

1 cup raisins

375ml (13 fl oz) good-quality sherry

6 medium zucchini

6 quail, deboned and butterflied

olive oil

salt/freshly ground black pepper

2 tablespoons (40g/1½ oz) unsalted butter

1 cup basil leaves, torn

½ cup (125g/4½ oz) pine nuts, toasted

¼ cup chives, chopped

jus (Basics page 159)

12 slices pancetta, grilled

Soak raisins in sherry overnight.

Using a mandoline, 'spaghetti' slice zucchini. Set aside.

Heat a ridged grill or large heavy-based pan over high heat. Brush quail with olive oil and season. Place skin-side down on grill or hot pan to sear until good colour is achieved. Turn quail and continue to cook until pink. Remove from pan and allow to rest briefly.

Meanwhile, place another pan over high heat, lightly oil and quickly stir-fry the zucchini until slightly wilted. Add butter, basil, pine nuts, soaked raisins and chives; sauté briefly.

To serve, place a portion of hot zucchini mixture in centre of each plate and top with a quail. Drizzle over a little hot jus and top each with 2 slices of pancetta.

Note: Zucchini is best sautéed in two batches as too much heat is lost when all is wilted in one pan.

Honey-glazed quail, beetroot, apple & hazelnuts

Serves 6

People often comment on our dressings and vinaigrettes, wanting to know what the secret ingredient is. But there is no secret; it is usually just a matter of using good vinegars and great oils.

This dressing is quite flexible. If you cannot find Champagne vinegar, by all means use a good-quality white wine vinegar. The hazelnut oil can be substituted with walnut if you prefer. Walnuts would also work well in the salad.

6 large quail, boned and butterflied

olive oil

salt/freshly ground black pepper

2 tablespoons (40ml/1¹/₂ fl oz) good-quality honey

Beetroot

12 baby beetroot

1 cup (250ml/9 fl oz) Champagne vinegar

1 cup (250g/9 oz) brown sugar

good pinch of salt

water

Dressing

100ml (3¹/₂ fl oz) citrus juice (1 lemon or 1–2 oranges)

1 tablespoon (20ml) Champagne vinegar

300ml (10¹/₂ fl oz) extra-virgin olive oil

2 tablespoons (40ml/1¹/₂ fl oz) hazelnut oil

2 teaspoons (10 ml) Dijon mustard

1 clove garlic, chopped (optional)

salt/freshly ground black pepper

Salad

2 Granny Smith apples, unpeeled, cored, cut into matchsticks

12 sprigs celery leaves (from heart)

100g (3¹/₂ oz) watercress, washed and spun

¹/₂ red onion, finely sliced into rings

³/₄ cup whole hazelnuts, toasted and skinned

To cook beetroot, place in a large saucepan with vinegar, sugar and salt. Cover with water. Bring to the boil, then simmer until tender. Allow to cool in cooking liquor. Remove beetroot, reserving liquor. Peel and halve beetroot and store in liquor.

To make dressing, whisk together all ingredients in a bowl. Season to taste with salt and pepper.

To make salad, combine all ingredients in a large bowl with enough dressing to moisten.

To cook quail, heat a large, heavy-based frying pan over high heat. Brush quail with olive oil and season. Place skin-side down in hot pan and sear until good colour is achieved. Turn over and continue to cook until pink (medium). Brush with honey then remove from pan and allow to rest briefly. Divide each quail into 2 breasts and 2 legs.

To serve, place about 5 pieces of beetroot in centre of each plate. Place 1 leg and 1 breast of quail on base of each plate. Pile a generous handful of salad on top of quail. Arrange another breast and leg on top of salad. Spoon a little beetroot cooking liquor around plate.

Lamb loin, chickpeas, ruby chard & minted yoghurt

Serves 6

3 lamb loins, approximately 700g (1¹/₂ lb), denuded (silver skin removed)

¹/₄ cup (60ml/2 fl oz) olive oil

2 cloves garlic, finely chopped

1 tablespoon fresh thyme leaves, finely chopped

salt/freshly ground black pepper

¹/₄ cup picked mint leaves, sliced

1 cup (250ml/9 oz) natural or Greek-style yoghurt

Spiced chickpeas

2 x 400g (14 oz) cans whole peeled tomatoes

olive oil

1 medium onion, diced

3 cloves garlic, thinly sliced

1 medium carrot, peeled, cut in half lengthways then sliced on the diagonal

¹/₂ red chilli, julienned

1 pinch hot chilli flakes

¹/₂ teaspoon cumin, freshly roasted and ground

1 tablespoon fresh thyme leaves, chopped

1 bay leaf

2 teaspoons (10ml) tomato paste

salt/freshly ground black pepper

1 x 400g (14 oz) can chickpeas, drained and rinsed

¹/₂ cup (60ml/2 fl oz) dry white wine

juice of half a lemon

50g (2 oz) baby chard or ruby chard

small handful flat-leaf parsley leaves

jus (Basics page 159)

12 oven-roasted tomato halves (Basics page 167)

Marinate lamb in combined oil, garlic and thyme overnight.

To prepare the chickpeas, crush tomatoes by hand and discard most of the seeds and juice. Reserve tomato flesh.

Heat a saucepan with just enough olive oil to cover the base. Add onions and garlic and sweat until onion is transparent.

Add carrot, chilli, chilli flakes, cumin, thyme, bay leaf and tomato paste. Season with salt and pepper. Cook for several minutes and add reserved tomatoes, chickpeas and wine. Continue to cook over low heat for 10–15 minutes, skimming if necessary. Remove from heat and check seasoning.

Preheat oven to 220°C (425°F).

Remove lamb from marinade. Heat a wide, heavy-based frying pan over high heat until very hot. Season with salt and pepper. Seal in hot pan until good colour is achieved. Place in hot oven for 8–10 minutes and cook until pink (medium). Remove lamb from pan and allow to rest for 5 minutes before slicing.

To serve, gently warm chickpeas. Add lemon juice and stir in chard and parsley. Warm through until chard just wilts.

Place spiced chickpeas in centre of 6 warm serving plates. Slice each loin diagonally into 4 long strips. Arrange slices on top of chickpeas. Drizzle jus over lamb and around plate. Mix mint and yoghurt and spoon over. Finish with warm oven-roasted tomatoes.

Fried Gympie goat's cheese, baby beets, rocket & pecans

Serves 6

Gympie, 1 hour north of Brisbane, is where Camille Mortaud produces brilliant goat's cheese, both fresh and mature. We use the mature one for this recipe because it is firmer and does not melt during frying. The cheese is cylindrical in shape, approximately 7cm (2³/₄ in) high and 5cm (2 in) in diameter. You can use a different shape, but the small discs suit this recipe.

240g (8¹/₂ oz) mature Gympie goat's cheese
  (approximately 2 logs)
water
plain flour for dusting
olive oil

Beetroot

12 baby beetroot
1 cup (250ml/9 fl oz) Champagne vinegar
1 cup (250g/9 oz) brown sugar
good pinch salt
water

Salad

75g (2¹/₂ oz) rocket, washed
75g (2¹/₂ oz) baby beetroot leaves, washed
1 red onion, thinly sliced
¹/₂ cup (125g/4¹/₂ oz) pecans
salt/freshly ground black pepper
red wine vinaigrette (Basics page 161)

To cook beetroot, place in a large saucepan with vinegar, sugar and salt. Cover with water. Bring to the boil and simmer until tender. Allow to cool. Remove beetroot, reserving liquor. Peel and halve beetroot and store in liquor.

To cook cheese, using a hot knife, carefully cut each log into 6, giving you 12 slices. Dip each slice in water then dust with flour. Place a non-stick frying pan over medium heat. Add a little olive oil to the pan and, when hot, fry several cheese slices until golden. Turn and cook other side. Remove from pan, drain on kitchen paper and fry remaining cheese. Keep warm.

To make salad, place ingredients in a bowl. Toss with enough vinaigrette to moisten.

To serve, divide salad between 6 plates, placing 2 slices goat's cheese and 4 beetroot halves, at room temperature, alongside salad.

Pan-fried quail with mascarpone, chickpeas & roasted tomatoes

Serves 6

6 quail, deboned and butterflied

olive oil

salt/freshly ground black pepper

12 oven-roasted tomato halves (Basics page 167)

200g (7 oz) English spinach, washed, picked, stems removed

unsalted butter

jus (Basics page 159)

Chickpeas

250g (9 oz) dried chickpeas (Basics page 170) or 1 x 400g (14 oz) can chickpeas, drained and rinsed

2 teaspoons (10ml) tahini paste

juice of 1 lemon

3 tablespoons (60ml/2 fl oz) extra-virgin olive oil

2 cloves garlic, extra, crushed

salt/freshly ground black pepper

Filling

1/2 cup (125g/4 1/2 oz) mascarpone

grated zest of 1 lemon

fresh thyme leaves, chopped

freshly ground black pepper

1 egg yolk

If using dried chickpeas, prepare chickpeas as recipe directs.

Drain prepared chickpeas, reserving half the cooking liquor, and divide chickpeas into two batches. Place one half in a food processor and blend with tahini, lemon juice, oil, extra garlic and enough of the cooking liquor to form a smooth paste. Combine remaining chickpeas with chickpea paste. Season to taste.

To make filling, combine all ingredients in a bowl.

Place a heaped teaspoonful of filling under skin of each quail, then refrigerate until required.

When ready to serve, preheat oven to 220°C (425°F). Heat an ovenproof pan over high heat and brush lightly with oil.

Season quail and place skin-side up in the hot pan and sear the underside. Turn quail over and place pan in oven for approximately 5 minutes. When cooked, remove from pan and rest for several minutes.

Meanwhile, warm oven-roasted tomatoes. Wilt spinach in a hot pan with a little butter, salt and pepper.

To serve, place chickpea mixture in centre of each warmed plate and top with spinach. Place tomatoes to one side, then quail on top of spinach. Drizzle warmed jus over and around.

Pressed duck & potato terrine with bitter greens & red onion jam

Serves 12–14

12 duck legs, slow roasted (Basics page 163)
1 bulb roasted garlic (Basics page 168)
6 whole cabbage leaves
300ml (10$\frac{1}{2}$ fl oz) cream
1 bunch fresh thyme, chopped
$\frac{1}{2}$ whole nutmeg, grated
salt/freshly ground black pepper
3 large potatoes, peeled and thinly sliced

lemon dressing (Basics page 160)
assorted mixed leaves, such as radicchio, frisèe, witlof
fresh herbs such as snipped chives or picked chervil
red onion jam (Basics page 166)
6 slices ciabatta, drizzled with olive oil
  and toasted

Prepare slow roasted duck and roasted garlic as recipes direct. Preheat oven to 200°C (400°F).

Blanch cabbage leaves in salted boiling water, then drain and refresh in iced water. Drain well. Cut stems from leaves.

Heat cream in a saucepan with thyme, nutmeg, salt and pepper. Bring to the boil. Remove from heat. Layer potato slices in an ovenproof dish and cover with cream mixture. Cover with foil and bake for 30 minutes or until potatoes are tender. Allow to cool slightly.

Line a Le Creuset or similar loaf pan approximately 30cm (12 in) x 10cm (4 in) wide x 8cm (3 in) high with plastic wrap, allowing 3–4cm (approximately 1$\frac{1}{2}$ in) overhang. Then line with cabbage leaves, allowing the same overhang.

Briefly warm duck legs, remove and discard skin and bones. Break flesh into a large bowl. Squeeze over roasted garlic cloves. Season with pepper, but only a little salt.

Using a slotted spoon, lift enough potatoes from the oven dish to cover the base of the loaf pan in a single layer. Place a layer of duck on top of potatoes. Repeat this process until the terrine is full. Discard excess cream from potatoes. Fold over cabbage leaves to completely enclose the terrine. Cover with overhanging plastic wrap.

Place a small cutting board or similar flat object on top of terrine and press gently to compress. Place a heavy weight on top of cutting board while terrine is cooling in refrigerator overnight.

To serve, bring terrine to room temperature and cut into 1–1$\frac{1}{2}$cm ($\frac{1}{2}$in) slices. Place a slice of terrine in the centre of each plate. Dress mixed leaves and herbs with lemon dressing and arrange salad beside terrine. Serve with warm red onion jam and toasted ciabatta.

Potato gnocchi with braised oxtail

Serves 6

Gnocchi can be used in many ways. In my first book we had a wonderful vegetarian dish which is served with gorgonzola, spinach and pine nuts. It can be fried as in this recipe, which I really like because it is crispy on the outside, or simply reheated in boiling water. This dish would also be great with braised lamb or veal shank in place of the oxtail.

potato gnocchi (Basics page 170)

braised oxtail (Basics page 169)

olive oil

10 golden shallots, peeled and sliced

2 cloves garlic, crushed

1 carrot, diced

1 stick celery, diced

1 leek, halved lengthwise, diced and
 washed well

2 teaspoons thyme leaves, chopped

Prepare gnocchi as recipe directs and set aside.

Prepare braised oxtail as recipe directs and cool to room temperature. Remove all meat from bones, discarding sinew, bone and fat. Reserve meat and cooking liquor separately.

Heat oil in a pan and sauté shallots, garlic, carrot, celery, leek and thyme until lightly coloured.

In a separate pan, heat reserved oxtail cooking liquor and reduce by half, until it is rich and glossy.

Add some of the reduced liquor to sautéed vegetables. Add reserved oxtail meat and heat through.

In a large frying pan, gently sauté gnocchi until hot and lightly golden. Pour over hot meat and vegetable sauce.

Serve in shallow bowls, allowing 5 pieces gnocchi per person for an entrée.

Prawn linguine with spinach, tomato, coriander & lemon

Serves 6

500g (1 lb) linguine (or spaghetti)

olive oil

20 prawns, cleaned, heads removed, tails left on

2 teaspoons unsalted butter

2 teaspoons salted capers, well rinsed

1 cup (250g/9 oz) tomato skinned and diced

1 lemon, skinned and segmented over a bowl to catch juice

150g (5 oz) English spinach, washed, picked, stems removed

1/2 cup flat-leaf parsley, washed

salt/freshly ground black pepper

1/2 cup (125g/4 1/2 oz) grated parmesan

small handful fresh coriander leaves, washed and spun

Heat a heavy-based pan, add a little olive oil, then increase heat to very high and sauté prawns. This may need to be done in two batches to avoid stewing.

Cook linguine in boiling, salted water until al dente.

Meanwhile, heat a separate pan and add butter, capers, tomato and lemon segments and juice. Fold in spinach and parsley.

Drain linguine and add to pan. Stir through prawns. Check seasoning and adjust if necessary.

Spoon linguine and prawns into 6 large serving bowls, top with a little parmesan, coriander leaves and a good grinding of black pepper.

Pumpkin cannelloni with carrot & lemongrass broth

Serves 6

The pumpkin must be a dry variety; if the filling is too moist the cannelloni will lose their shape. We use Queensland Blue or Jarrahdale. The carrots must be freshly juiced. If you do not have a juicer, Health Food shops should be able to supply you with some fresh juice. Always use on the date of purchase. In this recipe we have specified using lasagne sheets. At the restaurant we make our own pasta, but for home it is probably considerable effort to obtain just 6 sheets.

6 lasagne sheets

3 cups julienned leek, carrot and celery

knob unsalted butter

salt/freshly ground black pepper

few sprigs chervil

Pumpkin filling

1 small pumpkin or 1/2 large pumpkin, washed, skin on

6–8 fresh sage leaves

1 bulb garlic, cut in half

extra-virgin olive oil

salt/freshly ground black pepper

1/2 cup (125g/4 1/2 oz) grated parmesan

2 tablespoons (40g/1 1/2 oz) mascarpone

2 teaspoons chopped fresh sage leaves, extra

Cook lasagne sheets in boiling salted water until tender. Refresh in iced water and pat dry with a clean, dry tea towel. Set aside.

To make pumpkin filling, preheat oven to 160°C (325°F).

Roughly cut pumpkin into large pieces, leaving skin intact but removing seeds. Place pumpkin in a bowl with sage, garlic, a good splash of olive oil, salt and pepper. Lay pumpkin on a non-stick tray or a baking tray lined with non-stick baking (silicone) paper.

Place in oven and slow roast for 40–50 minutes or until tender when tested with a knife. Allow to cool.

Scrape pumpkin from skin and discard skin, sage and garlic. If pumpkin looks quite wet, place in a non-stick frying pan and gently dry out, stirring continuously over low heat for several minutes to remove excess moisture.

Place pumpkin into a bowl and combine with parmesan, mascarpone and extra sage. Check seasoning.

Continued overleaf

Carrot & lemongrass broth

1 kg (2 lb) carrots, washed, peeled and trimmed

2 sticks lemongrass, roughly chopped

1 red chilli, halved

2 kaffir lime leaves

few sprigs mint

few sprigs coriander

lime juice to taste (2–3 limes)

pinch sugar

$^1/_2$ cup (125ml/4$^1/_2$ fl oz) softly whipped cream

To make broth, juice carrots. You should have approximately 600ml (1 pint) juice. Reserve 100ml (3$^1/_2$ fl oz) and place remaining 500ml (18 fl oz) juice in a heavy-based saucepan with lemongrass and chilli.

Over a moderate heat, reduce juice by half (250ml/9 fl oz). Remove from heat and add kaffir lime leaves, mint and coriander. Allow to infuse for 30 minutes.

When cool, add remaining carrot juice and lime juice, and adjust seasoning with sugar, salt and pepper. Strain and set aside.

To assemble, lay lasagne sheets out. Fill with pumpkin filling and roll up to achieve a cylinder shape approximately 12cm (4$^1/_2$ in) in length and 3cm (1$^1/_2$ in) in diameter. To reheat, either place in a steamer 5–8 minutes to heat through or in an oiled earthenware dish covered with foil in a moderate oven 10–15 minutes to heat through.

To serve, toss julienned vegetables in butter with salt and pepper in a non-stick pan over moderate heat until cooked but still firm.

Bring carrot and lemongrass broth back to the boil. Using a Bamix, blend in cream to give a slightly foamy consistency.

In the centre of 6 shallow bowls, divide the sautéed vegetables. Place a hot cannelloni on each mound of vegetables. Ladle carrot and lemongrass broth around cannelloni. Garnish with chervil.

This dish can also be garnished with some fine strips of ginger that have been fried until crisp.

Right: Pumpkin cannelloni with carrot & lemongrass broth (recipe page 43)

Left: Grilled quail, zucchini, pine nuts, sherry-soaked raisins & basil (recipe page 35)

Right: Lamb loin, chickpeas, ruby chard & minted yoghurt (recipe page 37)

Left: Honey-glazed quail, beetroot,
apple & hazelnuts
(see page 36)

Gympie goat's cheese,
rocket & pecans

Left: Pressed duck & potato terrine with bitter greens & red onion jam (recipe page 40)

Right: Salad of prosciutto, grilled pears, hazelnuts & gorgonzola (recipe page 58)

Salad of spinach, peas, mint & warm goat's cheese crostini

Serves 6

This is one of my favourite salads. Its flavour relies entirely on the freshness of the ingredients, so I would not recommend attempting it unless you can obtain fresh peas and herbs in pristine condition.

lemon dressing (Basics page 160)

150g (5 oz) fresh spinach leaves, washed well

1 cup freshly podded peas, blanched briefly in boiling salted water, refreshed in iced water and drained

1 cup sugar snap peas, blanched briefly in boiling salted water, refreshed in iced water and drained

1/2 cup fresh basil leaves, washed

1/2 cup fresh mint leaves, washed

1/2 cup flat-leaf parsley leaves, washed

2 tablespoons green (spring) onion, sliced

Crostini

12 slices French stick, cut diagonally in 1 1/2 cm (approximately 1/2 in) thick slices, approximately 20cm (8 in) in length

180g (6 oz) goat's cheese (or fresh goat's curd)

extra-virgin olive oil

freshly ground black pepper

Prepare lemon dressing as recipe directs.

In a large bowl, combine spinach, peas, basil, mint, parsley and onion. Toss with enough lemon dressing to moisten.

Toast bread slices under hot grill, then spread with goat's cheese. Reduce grill to low setting and warm through.

To serve, place salad in the centre of each plate. Place 2 goat's cheese crostini beside each salad, drizzle a little oil over goat's cheese and grind over black pepper.

Left: Salad of spinach, peas, mint & warm goat's cheese crostini

Grilled quail, wild mushroom orecchiette, parsley, garlic & lemon

Serves 6

Orecchiette (meaning "little ears") is a cup-shaped pasta that holds a lot more sauce than penne or other pasta shapes.

6 quail, deboned and butterflied

olive oil

salt/freshly ground black pepper

250g (9 oz) orecchiette pasta (preferably Italian)

400g (14 oz) mixed fresh mushrooms (such as morels, swiss browns, slippery jacks), sliced

2 cloves garlic, chopped

juice of 1 lemon

$^1/_2$ cup flat-leaf parsley, finely sliced

Sauce

60g (2 oz) dried porcini mushrooms

olive oil

2 medium shallots (French shallots), finely sliced

1 clove garlic, finely chopped

750ml (1$^1/_3$ pints) mushroom stock (Basics page 159)

300ml (10$^1/_2$ fl oz) pouring cream (35% butterfat)

To make the sauce, soak dried porcini mushrooms in enough warm water to cover, and stand for 1 hour to rehydrate. Remove rehydrated porcini from liquid. Strain liquid through a muslin cloth and reserve. Thinly slice porcini. In a heavy-based pan, heat olive oil and sauté shallots and garlic until transparent. Add porcini and continue to cook until tender. Remove from pan.

Deglaze pan with reserved porcini liquid then transfer to a large stainless steel saucepan. Add mushroom stock and sautéed porcini and shallots. Bring to the boil and reduce by two-thirds. The sauce should have a glaze-like consistency. Add cream, bring to the boil, reduce again by one quarter. Adjust seasoning to taste.

Cook pasta in boiling salted water until al dente. Drain, refresh and set aside.

To cook the quail, heat a large ridged grill or heavy-based frying pan over high heat. Brush quail with a little olive oil and season. Place skin-side down on grill or hot pan to sear until good colour is achieved. Turn and continue to cook until pink. Remove from pan and allow to rest briefly.

To cook the mushrooms, place another pan with a little olive oil over high heat and lightly sauté mixed mushrooms. Add garlic and sauté briefly until tender, then deglaze pan with lemon juice to taste. Add porcini sauce and return to the boil.

Reheat cooked pasta in boiling salted water. Drain and add to sauce with parsley. Adjust seasoning to taste.

To serve, divide combined pasta and sauce between six bowls. Top each plate of pasta with a quail.

Roast rabbit, wet polenta, white onions, asparagus & herb mascarpone

Serves 6

6 rabbit legs (hindquarter), thigh bone removed
6 thyme sprigs
2 heads garlic, halved
salt/freshly ground black pepper
500ml (18 fl oz) olive oil
500ml (18 fl oz) vegetable oil
wet polenta (Basics page 167)

White onions & asparagus

12 small spring onion bulbs
1 tablespoon (20g) unsalted butter
100ml (3^1/$_2$ fl oz) chicken stock (Basics page 158)
12 spears asparagus, cut in half
300ml (10^1/$_2$ fl oz) jus (Basics page 159)

Herb mascarpone

500g (1 lb) mascarpone
3 heads garlic confit (Basics page 168)
1^1/$_2$ cups chopped herbs such as parsley, thyme, sage, chervil
salt/freshly ground black pepper

Preheat oven to 150°C (300°F).

Spread rabbit legs across the base of a deep baking tray large enough to just fit them in. Add thyme sprigs and garlic heads and season well.

Warm both oils in a saucepan over medium heat. Pour over enough oil to just cover rabbit legs.

Cover with foil and place in the oven. Cook slowly for 1–1^1/$_2$ hours until tender.

Prepare wet polenta as recipe directs.

To make herb mascarpone, place mascarpone in a bowl. Squeeze in garlic confit and add herbs. Season well with salt and pepper.

To make the white onions and asparagus, in a small pan, sauté spring onion bulbs in butter with salt and pepper. Add stock and bring to the boil. Turn down heat to simmer gently until onions are tender and stock has reduced. Add asparagus and simmer for another minute to cook and glaze vegetables with chicken stock.

To serve, place a generous spoonful of polenta slightly off-centre on each plate. Place glazed vegetables off-centre beside polenta. Lean a rabbit leg between vegetables and polenta. Spoon herbed mascarpone on top of rabbit and drizzle over some jus.

Salad of roast quail, parsnips, pear, hazelnuts & verjuice

Serves 6

This is a lovely fresh salad that was included in Maggie Beer's book Cooking with Verjuice. Verjuice is the juice of unripe grapes and can be used in place of vinegar or citrus in vinaigrettes. It is also good for finishing sauces or when cooking poultry or seafood. Verjuice has a tart and slightly acidic taste with the subtle flavour of grapes.

6 large quail, boned
olive oil
salt/freshly ground black pepper

Parsnips

6 medium parsnips, peeled, halved, cores removed
few sprigs thyme
5 cloves garlic, unpeeled, lightly crushed
olive oil

Verjuice vinaigrette

100ml (3$^1/_2$ fl oz) verjuice (Glossary)
juice of 1 lemon
2 teaspoons (10g) seeded mustard
1 tablespoon thyme leaves, chopped
150ml (5 fl oz) light olive oil
150ml (5 fl oz) extra-virgin olive oil
salt/freshly ground black pepper

Salad

2 witlof, leaves separated
100g (3$^1/_2$ oz) frisée or rocket, washed and spun
$^1/_2$ red onion, finely sliced
$^1/_2$ cup flat-leaf parsley, picked and washed
$^3/_4$ cup (185g/6$^1/_2$ oz) hazelnuts, roasted, skinned and roughly chopped
3 ripe but firm pears, cored and sliced

To roast parsnips, preheat oven to 180°C (350°F). In a bowl, combine parsnips, thyme, garlic and a little olive oil. Mix well to coat, then place parsnips on a non-stick oven tray and roast until tender. Set aside until required.

To make vinaigrette, place verjuice, lemon juice, mustard and thyme in a bowl. Whisk in combined oils, then season to taste with salt and pepper.

To make salad, mix together all ingredients in a large bowl. Dress with enough vinaigrette to moisten.

Increase oven temperature to 200°C (400°F). Heat a heavy-based ovenproof frying pan over high heat. Brush quail with olive oil and season with salt and pepper. Place skin-side down in pan to sear until a good colour is achieved. Turn quail and place pan in preheated oven. Roast for 4–5 minutes. Remove from pan and allow to rest briefly. Divide each quail into 2 breasts and 2 legs.

To serve, reheat parsnips and arrange on the base of each plate. Place 1 quail leg and 1 breast on top of parsnips. Arrange a generous handful of salad on top of quail. Place another breast and leg on top of salad. Drizzle a little extra vinaigrette over and around.

Salad of Peking duck, bean shoots, coriander & mint

Serves 6

Chinese roasted ducks are readily available in Chinatown. Although the proprietor will probably offer to cut up the duck for you, opt for a whole one.

2 Chinese roasted ducks

1/4 cup Asian fried shallots

3 tablespoons sesame seeds, toasted

Dressing

1/4 cup (60ml/ 2 fl oz) hoisin sauce

1/4 cup (60ml/2 fl oz) soy sauce

1/4 cup (60 ml/2 fl oz) honey

Salad

1/2 wombok (Chinese cabbage), shredded

1 cup bean shoots

1/2 cup Vietnamese mint leaves

1/2 cup mint leaves

1 cup coriander leaves

1/2 cup green (spring) onions, sliced diagonally

1 cup (250g/9 oz) toasted cashews

1 chilli, seeds removed, finely sliced lengthwise

Remove meat in large pieces from ducks. Place skin-side up on a lightly greased baking tray. Preheat oven grill to high.

To make the dressing, whisk all ingredients together.

To make the salad, gently toss all ingredients together in a large bowl. Combine with enough dressing to moisten.

To serve, place duck pieces under grill until skin is crispy and duck is warmed through. Divide salad between 6 plates. Place several duck pieces on top of salad. Sprinkle with fried onions and sesame seeds. Drizzle a little dressing over duck and around salad.

Salad of prosciutto, grilled pears, hazelnuts & gorgonzola

Serves 6

When buying prosciutto, always make sure it is sliced as thinly as possible – there is nothing worse than thick slices of prosciutto. Jonathon's of Collingwood in Melbourne produce a fantastic prosciutto, along with many other smallgoods, which are available Australia-wide.

5 ripe but firm pears

extra-virgin olive oil

knob of unsalted butter

1/2 cup (125g/4 1/2 oz) hazelnuts, roasted, skinned and roughly chopped

180g (6 oz) gorgonzola

120g (4 oz) wild rocket, washed and picked

18 slices prosciutto, sliced very thinly

freshly ground black pepper

6 slices ciabatta (or similar crusty Italian bread)

Preheat oven to 200°C (400°F).

Leaving skins intact, cut pears into quarters and remove core. Heat a heavy-based pan with a little olive oil and sauté pears until slightly coloured. Remove pan from heat, add butter and place in oven for 5–8 minutes.

Remove from oven and drain pears on kitchen paper.

To serve, place 3 wedges of pear off-centre on each plate and sprinkle with hazelnuts. Place a spoonful of gorgonzola beside pears. Arrange rocket next to pear and gorgonzola. Loosely drape prosciutto on top. Drizzle prosciutto with olive oil and finish with a good grind of black pepper.

Drizzle ciabatta slices with olive oil and grill until well coloured on both sides. Serve with salad.

Salad of slow-cooked duck, roasted Jerusalem artichokes & radicchio

Serves 6

Jerusalem artichokes have a beige skin and look not dissimilar to fresh ginger. Although varied in size and shape, they are quite knobbly and often about the size of a golf ball. They have white flesh and a sweet, nutty flavour. There is no need to peel them.

6 confit duck legs (Basics page 163)

12 Jerusalem artichokes, washed

olive oil

salt/freshly ground black pepper

100g (3½ oz) radicchio leaves, picked and washed

100g (3½ oz) baby English spinach, stems removed, washed and spun

1 small red onion, thinly sliced

½ cup flat-leaf parsley leaves, picked

red wine vinaigrette (Basics page 161)

12 slices bacon, grilled until crisp, drained on kitchen paper

Prepare confit duck legs as recipe directs.

Cut artichokes in half and toss with olive oil, salt and pepper. Place on a baking tray and roast at 200°C (400°F) for 30–40 minutes or until golden and tender.

Heat duck legs under grill to warm through and achieve good colour on skin.

In a large salad bowl, combine radicchio, spinach, onion, parsley and enough red wine vinaigrette to moisten.

Using gloves or tongs, remove duck meat from bone and place in salad. Add warm artichokes and crisp bacon, and toss lightly.

To serve, divide salad between plates or alternatively leave in large bowl and let guests serve themselves.

Sand crab, charred sourdough, fennel & chilli oil

Serves 6

It is hard to buy ready-picked sand crab that has not been frozen, so it is probably a good idea to buy some whole cooked crabs and pick it yourself. Sand crabs and mud crabs both have reasonable recovery of meat. Not the greatest job, but worth the effort!

500g (1 lb) picked sand crab (or blue swimmer) meat

1/4 cup chopped chervil

1/4 cup chopped flat-leaf parsley

1/4 cup chopped chives

1/2 cup (125ml/41/2 fl oz) mayonnaise (Basics page 156)

grated zest of 1 lime

juice of 2 limes

salt/freshly ground black pepper

6 slices sourdough bread

extra-virgin olive oil

chilli oil (Basics page 157)

6 lemon wedges

Fennel salad

2 large fennel, outer leaves and core removed, finely sliced/shaved

1/4 cup fennel tips, reserved from fennel

1/2 red onion, finely sliced

1 tablespoon (20g) seeded mustard (preferably Hill Farm Mountain Pepper)

lemon dressing (Basics page 160)

To make fennel salad, combine fennel, fennel tips, onion and mustard in a bowl. Coat with enough lemon dressing to moisten. Set aside and allow flavours to infuse while preparing crab.

In a large bowl, combine crab meat, herbs, mayonnaise, lime zest and juice, salt and pepper.

Lightly drizzle sourdough with olive oil and char under grill or on a ridged pan.

To serve, place a large spoonful of crab in the centre of each plate. Arrange fennel salad alongside. Place a slice of sourdough on edge of plate. Drizzle chilli oil over and around crab. Serve with lemon wedges.

Sautéed cuttlefish with chilli tomato chutney, crème fraîche & toasted sourdough

Serves 6

Cuttlefish are cousins to squid and calamari. They vary in colour but often have a pinkish-brown skin. They are caught as a by-product of prawn trawling.

1kg (2 lb) cuttlefish, cleaned

olive oil for coating

salt/freshly ground black pepper

2 cups (500 ml/18 fl oz) chilli tomato chutney/chilli jam (Basics page 157)

12 basil leaves, chopped

crème fraîche

3 limes, halved

good-quality sourdough bread, sliced, toasted and halved

freshly ground black pepper

Prepare cuttlefish by removing top layer of skin or membrane. Using a very sharp knife, cut cuttlefish into thin strips lengthways. Drizzle enough olive oil over cuttlefish strips just to coat.

Heat a heavy-based frying pan over high heat. Season cuttlefish and add to hot pan. Quickly sear until strips are lightly coloured. Toss through chilli tomato chutney and basil.

To serve, divide cuttlefish between serving bowls. Garnish with a spoonful of crème fraîche, half a lime and a piece of toasted sourdough. Grind over black pepper and serve at once.

Sautéed prawns, grilled focaccia, tomatoes, peppers & basil

Serves 6

500ml (18 fl oz) rich tomato sauce (Basics page 165)

1 red and 1 yellow pepper (capsicum), roasted, peeled and thickly sliced (Basics page 164)

36 green (uncooked) medium prawns

olive oil

1 tablespoon (20g) unsalted butter

2 French shallots, sliced

2 cloves garlic, crushed

2 red chillies, seeds removed & thinly sliced

salt/freshly ground black pepper

4 medium tomatoes, blanched, skinned and roughly chopped

¼ cup sliced green (spring) onion

1 tablespoon salted capers, well rinsed

6 thick slices focaccia

1 cup basil leaves, torn

3 limes, halved

Prepare tomato sauce as recipe directs.

Prepare peppers as recipe directs.

Shell and devein prawns, leaving tails intact. Heat oil in a heavy-based pan over high heat, add prawns and sauté on both sides. Add butter, shallots, garlic and chillies. Season with salt and pepper. Continue to cook until prawns are pink and opaque. Remove from pan and set aside.

Add rich tomato sauce to pan and heat through. Add peppers, green (spring) onion, tomato and capers. Return prawns to pan along with any juices.

Place focaccia under a hot grill and toast until golden and crisp. Divide between plates. Spoon over prawns and tomato mixture. Scatter with basil leaves and serve with half a lime.

Scallop tarte tatin with red pepper essence

Serves 6

red pepper essence (Basics page 164)

9 witlof (Belgian endive)

olive oil

3 tablespoons (60g/2 oz) brown sugar

salt/freshly ground black pepper

unsalted butter, for preparing tart tins

6 x 10cm (4 in) circles butter puff pastry

30 scallops (5 per person)

2 tablespoons (40g/1½ fl oz) crème fraîche

basil leaves, finely sliced

Prepare red pepper essence as recipe directs. Set aside.

Slice witlof thinly. Heat a little olive oil in a shallow pan and quickly sauté witlof over high heat. When nearly cooked through, sprinkle with brown sugar and cook for a further two minutes. Season to taste with salt and pepper. Drain, then set aside to cool.

Butter six 10cm (4 in) tart tins (or foil pie tins) and place on an oven tray. Preheat oven to 220°C (425°F).

Distribute cooked witlof evenly between tart tins then place a circle of puff pastry on each tart.

Cook tarts for 10 minutes or until pastry is risen and cooked through. Remove tarts from oven.

Meanwhile, heat a non-stick pan over high heat. Rub scallops with olive oil, salt and pepper and place in hot pan. Sear until just cooked through.

To serve, invert each tart onto a serving plate. Arrange 5 scallops per person on top of witlof. Place a teaspoon of crème fraîche on scallops. Drizzle the red pepper essence around each tart and scatter with basil. Serve immediately.

Atlantic salmon with fennel & red onion à la grecque, green olives & salsa verde

Serves 6

Both the onion and fennel can be prepared ahead and stored for several days in the cooking liquor. Once the onions and fennel have been used, the cooking liquor from both can be used a second time.

6 x 120g (720g/1½ lb total) portions Atlantic salmon, skin on, scaled and pin-boned

salt/freshly ground black pepper

olive oil

18 large green olives

reserved fennel tips

½ cup picked and washed flat-leaf parsley

lemon dressing (Basics page 160)

salsa verde (Basics page 165)

seeded mustard (preferably Hill Farm Mountain Pepper)

6 wedges of lemon

Red onion pickling mixture

3 red onions

500ml (18 fl oz) good-quality white wine or Champagne vinegar

330g (11½ oz) caster sugar

4 cloves

1 teaspoon mustard seeds

1 teaspoon black peppercorns

1 teaspoon caraway seeds

good pinch salt

small knob ginger, washed and chopped

Fennel à la grecque

3 large fennel bulbs

1 litre (1¾ pints) water

125ml (4½ fl oz) olive oil

1 teaspoon coriander seeds

a few black peppercorns

good pinch salt

3 bay leaves

few sprigs thyme

juice of 2 lemons

To pickle onions, peel, leaving root attached. Cut each onion into 6 wedges.

Bring pickling ingredients to the boil in a saucepan. Place onions in mixture and simmer gently until tender. Allow to cool in cooking liquor.

To make fennel à la grecque, pick fennel tips and set aside for garnish. Clean off outside leaves. Cut each bulb into 6–8 wedges, depending on size of fennel.

Bring remaining ingredients to the boil in a saucepan. Place fennel in mixture and simmer gently until tender. Allow to cool in cooking liquor.

To cook salmon, season skin with salt and pepper. Heat a heavy-based or non-stick frying pan over high heat and add a little olive oil. Sear salmon, skin-side down, until a good colour is achieved. Reduce heat to moderate, turn salmon and cook for a further 3–5 minutes or until medium rare.

Remove onions and fennel from cooking liquor and drain. In a bowl, mix onions, fennel, olives, fennel tips and parsley. Moisten with lemon dressing.

To serve, divide salad between 6 plates. Rest salmon on top of salad. Finish with a generous spoonful of salsa verde and a teaspoon of seeded mustard. Garnish with a wedge of lemon.

Seared bug tails with pasta, asparagus, tomato & chilli

Serves 6

600g (1¼ lb) Moreton Bay or Balmain bug tails, shelled

500g (1 lb) spaghetti

18 spears asparagus, sliced diagonally

2 cups (500 ml/18 fl oz) chilli tomato chutney (Basics page 157)

1 cup basil leaves, torn

Leave bug tails whole unless very large then slice in half lengthways.

Cook spaghetti in plenty of boiling salted water until al dente. Refresh in cold water, drain and set aside.

Blanch asparagus in boiling salted water, drain and refresh in iced water.

Sear bug tails in hot pan until just cooked. Remove from pan. Add chilli tomato chutney and bring to boil, then add asparagus.

Return bugs to pan. Check seasoning and remove from heat. Reheat spaghetti in boiling water and drain. Divide between 6 deep bowls. Spoon over bug and asparagus sauce and garnish with torn basil leaves.

Seared calves liver with champ, roasted shallots & crisp bacon

Serves 6

When choosing calves liver, look for one that is pale pink as this indicates that the calf has not been fully weaned.

1 small calves liver

24 small French shallots, unpeeled

olive oil

6 sprigs of thyme

best-quality balsamic vinegar

champ (Basics page 166)

jus (Basics page 159)

12 slices bacon, grilled until crisp, drained on kitchen paper

salt/freshly ground black pepper

Prepare liver by removing membrane and sinews and slice thinly, allowing 2–3 slices per serving.

Toss shallots and thyme with a little olive oil, place on an oven tray and roast at 200°C (400°F) until cooked through. Allow to cool and peel off skin. Give them a good splash with vinegar. Set aside.

Prepare champ as recipe directs. Add shallots to jus and warm through. Reheat bacon.

To serve, heat a little olive oil in a heavy-based frying pan over very high heat. Add several slices liver at a time and season. Quickly sear, turning once; inside should still be pink. Repeat with remaining liver.

Meanwhile, place a generous spoonful of champ in centre of each plate. Lay several slices of liver on top of champ. Spoon shallots and jus over and around. Top with bacon.

Sautéed chicken livers, pancetta, garlic crostini & rocket

Serves 6

6 x 2cm ($^3/_4$ in) slices ciabatta

2 heads roasted garlic (Basics page 168)

olive oil

700g (1$^1/_2$ lb) chicken livers, cleaned and trimmed

400ml (14 fl oz) jus (Basics page 159)

chicken stock (Basics page 158)

$^1/_2$ cup chives, finely chopped

300g (10$^1/_2$ oz) rocket, well washed

12 slices pancetta, grilled until crisp

To make crostini, toast ciabatta slices on both sides. Spread each slice with roasted garlic. Set aside in a warm place.

Heat a large, heavy-based pan until smoking. Add oil and quickly sauté chicken livers on all sides.

Add jus and simmer, turning livers and cooking until pink (medium). If necessary, thin down sauce with a little chicken stock. Lastly, stir in chives.

To serve, place a warm garlic crostini in the centre of each plate and spoon a portion of the livers alongside. Divide the rocket between the plates, placing a pile on the opposite side of crostini. Top each portion with 2 slices crisp pancetta.

Salad of seared cuttlefish, green pawpaw, chilli, lime & cashews

Serves 6

If you can buy the cuttlefish already cleaned, scoring is the only preparation required. The cuttlefish can also be substituted with seared rare tuna for a great salad.

The Thai-style dressing in this recipe is very versatile. It can be used with both seafood and meat salads. When finishing the dressing, do not be afraid to adjust the seasoning around the Thai principles of sweet, sour and salt – if it is a little bit sweet, add some more lime, or vice versa, and if it needs a little extra salt, add a little extra fish sauce.

600g (1¼ lb) medium sized cuttlefish

2 tablespoons (40 ml/1½ fl oz) light olive oil or peanut oil

salt/freshly ground black pepper

½ cup Asian fried shallots

3 limes, halved

lime and palm sugar dressing (Basics page 161)

Salad

2–3 continental cucumbers, peeled, cut into fine strips

1 small green pawpaw, skin and seeds removed, sliced into fine julienne

2 green (spring) onions, finely sliced diagonally

1–2 red chillies, finely julienned

1 cup coriander sprigs, washed and picked

¼ cup mint leaves, washed

¼ cup toasted cashews, unsalted

Prepare cuttlefish by slicing lengthwise through body. Open body and remove insides, including cuttle bone. Pull skin and membrane away from flesh and discard with tentacles. Using a very sharp knife, score flesh into diamond pattern. Toss cuttlefish with olive oil and refrigerate until required.

Prepare lime and palm sugar dressing as recipe directs.

To make the salad, combine all ingredients in a bowl. Add enough dressing to moisten ingredients.

To cook the cuttlefish, heat a heavy-based frying pan (or barbecue) over high heat. Drain excess oil from cuttlefish and season with salt and pepper. Place cuttlefish scored side down in hot pan and cook until good colour is achieved, turning once.

To serve, place 2–3 pieces of cuttlefish in centre of each plate. Arrange salad on top of cuttlefish. Place piece of cuttlefish on top of salad. Drizzle extra dressing over cuttlefish and salad. Sprinkle with fried onions and serve with lime halves.

Right: Salad of seared cuttlefish, green pawpaw, chilli, lime & cashews

Left: Seared calves liver with champ, roasted shallots & crisp bacon (recipe page 66)

Right: Smoked quail with witlof, parsnip, pear & honey (recipe page 83)

Left: Seared scallops with Tuscan bread salad (recipe page 81)

Right: Hervey Bay scallops, potato gnocchi, roast pumpkin & sage (recipe page 80)

*Left: Sesame crumbed brains,
green beans, mustard mayo &
pancetta (recipe page 82)*

*Right: Atlantic salmon with fennel &
red onion à la grecque, green
olives & salsa verde
(recipe page 64)*

Steamed asparagus, egg yolk ravioli, truffle oil & reggiano parmesan

Serves 6

Wonton wrappers are available in Chinatown, usually fresh. The remaining wrappers can be frozen for a further use. For visual effect, we prefer to use the square ones, but they are also available in rounds.

1 packet wonton wrappers

1–2 tablespoons cornflour

water

6 eggs

30 asparagus spears, ends trimmed

knob of best-quality unsalted butter

salt/freshly ground black pepper

shaved reggiano parmesan

truffle oil

To make ravioli, lay out 6 wonton wrappers on a clean dry surface. Mix cornflour with a little cold water to form a smooth paste. Using a pastry brush, brush outer edges of each wrapper with cornflour mixture.

Crack an egg, being careful not to break yolk. Place yolk in centre of wonton wrapper, reserving white for another use. Place another wrapper over top of yolk and firmly press down to seal edges, again taking great care to avoid breaking yolk. Repeat process with remaining eggs. Ravioli may be refrigerated on non-stick baking (silicone) paper dusted with cornflour prior to use.

Bring a large pot of salted water to the boil. Blanch asparagus until tender and drain. Toss with butter, salt and pepper. Keep warm.

In another large pot of boiling salted water, cook ravioli for a maximum of 3 minutes. Remove ravioli with a slotted spoon and rest on a plate.

To serve, divide asparagus between plates. Place ravioli on top of asparagus. Rest shaved parmesan against ravioli and asparagus. Drizzle with truffle oil and finish with a good grind of black pepper.

Left: Steamed asparagus, egg yolk ravioli, truffle oil & reggiano parmesan

Seared cuttlefish & chorizo sausage with salad of chickpeas, tomatoes & chilli

Serves 6

300g (10¹/₂ oz) chorizo sausage (2–3 sausages depending on size)

650g (1¹/₄ lb) cuttlefish, medium sized

250g (9 oz) dried chickpeas (Basics page 170) or 1 x 400g (14 oz) can chickpeas, drained and rinsed

100g (3¹/₂ oz) mizuna (or similar), washed and spun

24 cherry tomatoes

2 medium red chillies, seeds removed, diced

1 cup flat-leaf parsley, roughly chopped

grated zest of 2 lemons

juice of 2 lemons

extra-virgin olive oil

salt/freshly ground black pepper

Prepare cuttlefish by slicing lengthwise through the body. Open body and remove insides, including the cuttle bone. Pull skin and membrane away from flesh and discard with tentacles. Using a very sharp knife, score flesh into diamond pattern. Drizzle liberally with olive oil and set aside.

Slice sausages into rounds, approximately 1cm (¹/₂ in) thick.

To prepare salad, in a bowl place chickpeas, mizuna, cherry tomatoes, chilli, parsley, lemon zest and lemon juice with a good drizzle of olive oil. Lightly toss together and divide between 6 plates, leaving salad relatively flat on base of plate.

Meanwhile, heat two large cast iron or non-stick fry pans on high heat. Season cuttlefish with salt and pepper and place cuttlefish scored-side down in both pans. Maintain on high heat and once some colour is achieved add chorizo sausage and continue to cook. Turn cuttlefish and sausage over to cook evenly on both sides.

Remove from pan and arrange approximately 3 or 4 pieces of cuttlefish and 4 or 5 slices of chorizo on top of salad.

Hervey Bay scallops, cos leaves, apple, cashews & curry vinaigrette

Serves 6

500g (1 lb) Hervey Bay scallops (or similar)

3 baby cos, outer leaves removed

4 Granny Smith apples

150g (5 oz) cashews, roasted

$\frac{1}{2}$ red onion, sliced into thin rounds

2 tablespoons chopped chives

olive oil

6 lemon wedges

Curry vinaigrette

125ml (4$\frac{1}{2}$ fl oz) peanut oil

2 teaspoons cumin, roasted

2 teaspoons coriander seed, roasted

1 cinnamon stick

2 bay leaves

$\frac{1}{2}$ head garlic

1 piece ginger, roughly chopped

2 teaspoons curry powder

125ml (4$\frac{1}{2}$ fl oz) vegetable oil

2 French shallots, roughly chopped

75ml (2$\frac{1}{2}$ fl oz) lemon juice

salt/freshly ground black pepper

To make curry vinaigrette, heat peanut oil over moderate heat for several minutes. Add cumin, coriander, cinnamon, bay leaves, garlic, ginger and curry powder. Increase heat to high and continue to cook for several minutes to infuse flavours.

Add vegetable oil and shallots and continue to cook on a low heat for a further 10 minutes. Remove from heat and allow to stand for 1 hour. Strain and discard aromatics.

To make vinaigrette, whisk lemon juice into infused oil and correct seasoning with salt and pepper. This vinaigrette will keep in refrigerator for several days.

Remove core and separate leaves from cos. Wash and spin. Slice apples into matchsticks leaving skin intact.

In a large bowl, combine cos leaves, apple, cashews, red onion and chives. Add enough curry vinaigrette to moisten salad.

To serve, evenly divide salad into centre of each plate.

Meanwhile, heat a heavy-based non-stick pan to very high heat. Season scallops with a little olive oil, salt and pepper. In batches quickly sear scallops on both sides until just cooked and still moist.

Place scallops on top of salad and serve with a good grind of black pepper and lemon wedges.

Hervey Bay scallops, potato gnocchi, roast pumpkin & sage

Serves 6

We use scallops from Hervey Bay, which is on the Queensland coast near Fraser Island, several hundred kilometres north of Brisbane. These particular scallops are quite large, approximately 4cm (1¹/₂ in) in diameter and 1¹/₂cm (¹/₂ in) thick, and they have a grey roe which is usually discarded.

potato gnocchi (Basics page 170)

2 tablespoons fresh sage, chopped

¹/₂ Queensland blue or jap pumpkin

olive oil

salt/freshly ground black pepper

2 teaspoons cumin, roasted and ground

¹/₂ cup (125ml/4¹/₂ fl oz) clarified butter (Basics page 155)

sage leaves, extra

500g (1 lb) Hervey Bay scallops (or similar)

6 lemon wedges

Prepare gnocchi as recipe directs. While stirring in egg, parmesan and nutmeg, add sage. Set aside.

Preheat oven to 200°C (400°F). Line a baking tray with non-stick baking (silicone) paper.

To prepare pumpkin, remove skin, discard seeds and cut into large dice. Place in a large bowl and drizzle with olive oil. Season with salt, pepper and cumin.

Spread pumpkin on baking tray and roast for 15–20 minutes or until cooked and some colour is achieved. Set aside.

Heat clarified butter in a heavy frying pan. Add sage leaves and cook until crisp, being careful not to burn leaves. Remove with a slotted spoon and drain on kitchen paper.

When ready to serve, preheat oven to 200°C (400°F). Heat a little olive oil in a non-stick ovenproof pan. Briefly sauté gnocchi then place in oven for 8–10 minutes, until warmed through and some colour is achieved. Reheat pumpkin if necessary.

Divide pumpkin evenly between 6 plates. Place 3–4 gnocchi on top of pumpkin. Meanwhile heat a heavy-based non-stick pan to very high heat. In batches, with a little olive oil, salt and pepper, quickly sear scallops on both sides until just cooked and still moist. Place scallops on top of gnocchi and pumpkin. Scatter over fried sage leaves. Finish with a good grind of black pepper and a wedge of lemon.

Seared scallops with Tuscan bread salad

Serves 6

30 medium-sized scallops, cleaned

olive oil

salt/freshly ground black pepper

spicy tomato vinaigrette (Basics page 160)

lemon wedges, to serve

Tuscan bread salad

$^1/_2$ loaf ciabatta or other good Italian bread, cut into large dice

extra-virgin olive oil

6 vine-ripened tomatoes, blanched and skinned

2 red and 2 yellow peppers (capsicums) roasted, peeled and sliced (Basics page 164)

1 red onion, thinly sliced

1 cup basil leaves

$^1/_2$ cup (125g/4$^1/_2$ oz) ligurian or kalamata olives

8 anchovy fillets, drained and halved lengthwise

1 tablespoon salted capers, well rinsed

To make salad, drizzle ciabatta with a little olive oil, place on a baking tray and cook in a moderate oven until golden but not too dry.

Halve tomatoes horizontally and quarter each half.

In a large bowl, combine tomatoes, peppers, onion, basil, olives, anchovies and capers. Dress with enough vinaigrette to moisten. Lastly, fold through toasted ciabatta.

To cook scallops, heat a little oil in a shallow frying pan over high heat. Season scallops and quickly sear on both sides, taking care not to overcook.

To serve, centre a portion of salad on each plate. Arrange 5 scallops around and on top of salad, drizzle over a little extra vinaigrette and serve with a wedge of lemon.

Sesame crumbed brains, green beans, mustard mayo & pancetta

Serves 6

Offal is often not cooked at home because someone in the family doesn't like it, but try this dish as it was one of our best sellers. People might enjoy an offal dish in a restaurant environment but wouldn't go to the trouble at home. This dish is relatively simple to make and has a great combination of textures and flavours.

9 lamb brains, soaked overnight in cold, salted water

1 carrot, peeled and roughly chopped

1 leek, green tips removed, washed and roughly chopped

1 stalk celery, roughly chopped

1 onion, peeled and roughly chopped

2 bay leaves

splash white vinegar

crushed black peppercorns

300g (10½ oz) French beans (stringless green), trimmed

jus (Basics page 159)

12 slices pancetta, grilled until crisp, drained on kitchen paper

1 cup (250ml/9 fl oz) milk

2 eggs

salt/freshly ground black pepper

1 cup (250g/9 oz) plain flour

2 cups breadcrumbs

2 tablespoons sesame seeds

light olive oil

Mustard mayo

¾ cup mayonnaise (Basics page 156)

1 heaped tablespoon (approximately 20g) seeded mustard

1 tablespoon chopped chives

To cook the brains, drain and place in a saucepan and cover with fresh, cold water. Add carrot, leek, celery, onion, bay leaves, vinegar, peppercorns and salt.

On a very low heat, bring to nearly boiling (do not boil). Remove from heat and allow brains to cool in this liquor. Once cool, remove and carefully trim into halves, discarding any connective tissue.

To crumb brains, whisk together milk, eggs and seasoning. Toss brains through flour, shaking off excess. Dip into egg wash then coat with combined breadcrumbs and sesame seeds. Set aside.

To make the mustard mayonnaise, prepare mayonnaise as recipe directs.

In a bowl mix together mayonnaise, mustard and chives.

In a shallow frying pan over moderate heat, fry brains in olive oil, turning regularly until crisp and golden. Drain on kitchen paper.

Blanch beans in boiling salted water and drain. To serve, place some beans in the centre of each plate. Drizzle with mustard mayo and arrange 3 brain halves on top. Drizzle with a little jus and top with crisp pancetta.

Smoked quail with witlof, parsnip, pear & honey

Serves 6

This dish was the highlight of a promotional lunch we held in conjunction with Glenfiddich Whisky, where the object was to match aged single malt whiskies with food. This dish was matched with a nip of neat Solera Reserve 15-year-old single malt, and the combination of the smoked quail, parsnip and pear was an unbelievably harmonious one.

3 medium parsnips, peeled

few sprigs thyme

3 cloves garlic, unpeeled, lightly crushed

olive oil

6 smoked quail (Rannoch Farm if available), at room temperature

3 firm pears

3 witlof, broken into leaves

$^1/_2$ cup flat-leaf parsley, picked and washed

Dressing

1 cup (250ml/9 fl oz) fresh orange juice

2 teaspoons (10ml) honey

juice of $^1/_4$ lemon

1 tablespoon (20 ml) extra-virgin olive oil

salt/freshly ground black pepper

Preheat oven to 180°C (350°F).

Cut parsnips into quarters lengthwise and remove cores. In a bowl, combine thyme, garlic and a little olive oil. Add parsnips and coat well. Place parsnips on oven tray and roast until tender. Set aside.

Cut each quail into quarters, removing any small bones but leaving the leg and wing bone intact. Set aside.

Cut each pear into 6 wedges and remove core. Heat a little olive oil over medium heat in a heavy-based frying pan. Add pear wedges and toss until tender and some colour is achieved. (Do not allow pears to become too soft. They may need a few minutes in a hot oven.)

Add witlof leaves to the pan with pears and continue to toss until leaves have slightly wilted. Fold through parsley.

To make dressing, in a saucepan, bring orange juice to the boil and reduce by two-thirds (leaving $^1/_3$ cup). Whisk in honey, lemon juice and oil. Season to taste.

To serve, reheat parsnips in moderate oven. Place 1 quail leg and 1 breast in the centre of each plate. Evenly divide parsnip, pear and witlof between plates, arranging over top of quail. Drizzle liberally with dressing. Place another leg and breast on top, and spoon over any remaining dressing.

Smoked salmon, chilli corncakes, watercress, avocado & citrus crème fraîche

Serves 6

Chilli corncakes

500g (1 lb) corn kernels, cut from the cob

olive oil

salt/freshly ground black pepper

50ml (20 fl oz) hot milk

30g (1 oz) plain flour

6 egg whites

¼ cup coriander, washed, picked and roughly
  chopped

2 chillies, seeds removed, finely sliced

1 tablespoon chives, chopped

2 avocados, sliced into wedges

1 chilli, seeds removed, finely sliced

150g (5 oz) watercress, washed and spun

½ red onion, sliced into rings

lemon dressing (Basics page 160)

400g (14 oz) smoked salmon

freshly ground black pepper

3 limes, halved

To make chilli corncakes, in a heavy-based saucepan sweat corn kernels in the olive oil with salt and pepper until tender but not coloured. Spread corn on a baking tray and set aside to cool.

Place half the corn with milk in a food processor and blend until smooth. Mix puréed corn with flour and remaining corn.

Whisk egg whites to firm peaks. Briskly whisk one-third of whites into corn mixture, then gently fold in remaining whites. Lastly fold in coriander, chilli and chives. Check seasoning.

Heat a little oil in a non-stick frying pan over moderate heat. Drop spoonfuls of corn mixture into pan to form approximately 10cm (4 in) circles. Cook for a few minutes until bases are coloured. Place corncakes under a medium grill for several minutes to set tops. Gently flip over and cook for a further couple of minutes in pan on stovetop. Place on a wire rack to cool.

Continued opposite

Citrus crème fraîche

1 cup (250ml/9 fl oz) crème fraîche
grated zest and juice of 1 lime
grated zest and juice of 1 lemon
hot water
salt/freshly ground black pepper

To make citrus crème fraîche, place crème fraîche in a bowl and stir in lime and lemon zest and juice with enough hot water to achieve a dropping consistency. Season to taste. (As crème fraîche sits, the acid will cause it to thicken, so a little more hot water may need to be added just prior to serving.)

To serve, warm corncakes in a moderate oven. Place a corncake in the centre of each plate. Place several wedges of avocado on top of corncake. Sprinkle over sliced chilli. In a bowl, combine watercress and onion with a little lemon dressing. Arrange on top of chilli and avocado wedges. Gently drape 3–4 slices of smoked salmon on top of watercress, being careful not to flatten salad. Drizzle citrus crème fraîche over and around. Finish with a good grinding of black pepper. Serve with half a lime.

Spinach & ricotta hotcakes, smoked salmon, cucumber & radish

Serves 6

100g (3¹/₂ oz) plain flour

¹/₄ teaspoon bicarbonate of soda

2 teaspoons baking powder

2 egg yolks

250ml (9 oz) buttermilk

salt/freshly ground black pepper

100g (3¹/₂ oz) English spinach, washed, drained and finely chopped

1 tablespoon flat-leaf parsley, chopped

1 tablespoon chives, chopped

2 tablespoons green (spring) onion, finely chopped

125g (4¹/₂ oz) ricotta

2 egg whites

olive oil

360g (12¹/₂ oz) smoked salmon

³/₄ cup (6¹/₂ fl oz) crème fraîche

6 teaspoons salmon pearls

Salad

2 continental cucumbers

3 Jerusalem artichokes, peeled, finely sliced

6 radishes, finely sliced

1 small red onion, finely sliced

2 witlof, leaves separated and washed

100g (3¹/₂ oz) watercress, washed

100ml (3¹/₂ fl oz) lemon dressing (Basics page 160)

To make hotcakes, sift flour, bicarbonate of soda and baking powder into a large bowl. Combine egg yolks with buttermilk, then whisk into dry ingredients until mixture is smooth and free of lumps.

Season well and add spinach, herbs and shallots. Crumble ricotta into batter, keeping it quite chunky.

Whisk egg whites until soft peaks form, then fold into batter.

Preheat grill or salamander to moderate.

On the stove, place a blini pan over a moderate heat and brush with olive oil. When hot, fill three-quarters of the blini pan with batter and cook until coloured on the underside. Place blini pan under the grill or salamander to cook the tops. (**Note:** If you don't have a blini pan, heat a heavy-based frying pan and spoon batter in 12cm (5 in) rounds. Turn hotcakes in frying pan to cook the other side).

Transfer hotcakes from the pan to a cake rack.

To make salad, using a vegetable peeler, peel and discard skin from cucumbers. Proceed to peel long strips of flesh from the length of cucumbers, moving around the sides of the cucumber until eventually only the core of seeds remains.

Combine cucumber strips with remaining salad ingredients in a bowl. Drizzle with enough lemon dressing to moisten.

To serve, warm hotcakes in the oven, being careful not to let them dry out. Place one hotcake in the centre of each plate. Place a handful of salad on top of each hotcake. Drape over slices of smoked salmon then place a spoonful of crème fraîche beside each hotcake. Finish by sprinkling salmon pearls over crème fraîche and salmon.

Tartlet of seared salmon, beans, red onion, tomato & olives

Serves 6

1 quantity savoury shortcrust pastry (Basics page 154)

600g (1¼ lb) salmon, cleaned, skinned, pinbones removed and cut into 1cm (½ in) dice

olive oil

salt/freshly ground black pepper

100ml (3½ fl oz) red wine vinaigrette (Basics page 161)

1 small red onion, sliced

120g (4 oz) green beans, blanched and cut diagonally into 2–3cm (1 in) lengths

12 cherry tomatoes, halved

12 anchovy fillets, cut in half

¾ cup kalamata olives, pitted and sliced

2 tablespoons salted capers, well rinsed

½ cup torn basil leaves

mixed salad leaves

extra-virgin olive oil

lemon juice

salt/freshly ground black pepper

Prepare pastry as recipe directs.

Roll out pastry and line six 6cm (2½ in) x 8cm (3 in) tart cases (preferably with removable bases).

Blind bake (Basics page 155), pricking the pastry rather than using weights. Fully cook the cases and set aside. Keep warm.

Prepare red wine vinaigrette as recipe directs.

Season salmon with salt and pepper. Heat a non-stick pan and when very hot, add a little olive oil and sear salmon for a few minutes until medium rare. Remove from pan.

In a large bowl, combine onion, beans, tomatoes, anchovies, olives, capers and basil leaves. Moisten with red wine vinaigrette.

Spoon half the salmon into the base of the warmed tartlet cases. Divide the dressed salad between the cases and top with the remaining salmon and a good grinding of black pepper.

Place salad leaves in a bowl and toss with extra-virgin olive oil, lemon juice, salt and pepper.

To serve, centre a tartlet on each plate. Arrange salad next to tartlet.

Tartlet of asparagus, goat's cheese, kalamata olives & basil

Serves 6

1 quantity savoury shortcrust pastry (Basics page 154)

$^3/_4$ cup (6$^1/_2$ fl oz) red onion jam (Basics page 166)

1 cup (250g/9 oz) kalamata olives, pitted

24 asparagus spears, trimmed and cut diagonally into 6cm (2$^1/_2$ in) lengths

knob of unsalted butter

salt/freshly ground black pepper

$^1/_2$ cup basil leaves, torn

300g (10$^1/_2$ oz) fresh goat's cheese

extra-virgin olive oil

Prepare pastry as recipe directs. Roll out pastry and line six 8cm (3 in) tart cases (preferably with removable bases). Blind bake, pricking the pastry rather than using weights (Basics page 155). Fully cook cases and set aside.

Place red onion jam and olives in base of pre-cooked tart cases. Warm through in oven.

Meanwhile, blanch asparagus briefly in boiling salted water. Drain, add butter and season with salt and pepper.

Remove tart cases from oven and place basil leaves on top of olives and onions. Divide the asparagus between the tart cases. Using a teaspoon, randomly spoon the goat's cheese in small amounts over asparagus. Finish with a drizzle of extra-virgin olive oil and a good grind of black pepper.

Thai coconut chicken with cashews, cucumber, chilli, lime & palm sugar

Serves 6

5–6 boneless, skinless chicken breasts
  (approximately 600g/1¼ lb total)

2 chillies, finely sliced, including seeds

4 coriander roots and stems, roughly chopped

1 tablespoon ginger, peeled and grated

1 stick lemongrass, bruised, roughly chopped

3 kaffir lime leaves

2 x 400g (14 oz) cans coconut milk

400ml (14 fl oz) water

lime and palm sugar dressing (Basics page 161)

3 tablespoons Asian fried shallots

1 cup coriander leaves, picked and washed

Salad

2 continental cucumbers

½ cup mint leaves, picked

1 cup basil leaves, picked and washed

3 fresh chillies, seeds removed, finely sliced
  lengthwise

1 cup whole cashews, toasted

2 green (spring) onions, sliced diagonally

Place chicken breasts in a bowl. Add chillies, coriander, ginger, lemongrass and lime leaves. Rub well into chicken. Cover and refrigerate for several hours or preferably overnight.

To cook the chicken, in a large pan bring the coconut milk and water to the boil. Add marinated chicken breasts and simmer for approximately 12 minutes or until just cooked, but still moist. Allow to cool in coconut milk.

To make the salad, using a potato peeler, randomly take several slices of cucumber skin off and discard. Continue to slice long strips of cucumber with potato peeler, stopping just before you reach the seeds on each side. Toss together with remaining salad ingredients.

To serve, remove chicken from coconut milk and slice each breast lengthwise into long, thin strips. Divide approximately one-third of the slices between the plates and drizzle with 1–2 tablespoons of coconut poaching liquid.

Combine remaining chicken slices with salad and moisten with lime and palm sugar dressing. Place a generous portion of salad on top of chicken slices. Finish with fried onion and coriander leaves.

Tomato, olive & anchovy tarte tatin

Serves 6

9 roma tomatoes
1/2 cup (125g/4 1/2 oz) pitted kalamata olives
red onion jam (Basics page 166)
6 x 10cm (4 in) circles butter puff pastry
1 egg, beaten
12 anchovies
60g (2 oz) rocket, washed and spun
lemon dressing (Basics page 160)
best-quality balsamic vinegar

Lightly grease six 10cm (4 in) tart tins or blini pans. Preheat oven to 220°C (425°F).

Quickly blanch tomatoes in boiling water and refresh in iced water. Remove skins and place tomatoes on kitchen paper to drain. Cut in half.

Place 3 tomato halves in base of each tart tin, cut-side up. Sprinkle over olives. Spread a good tablespoon of red onion jam on top of tomatoes and olives. Top with puff pastry circles and brush with beaten egg.

Place tart tins on baking tray and cook until pastry is golden and has risen. Remove from oven and allow to sit for several minutes.

To serve, carefully invert each tart onto centre of plates. Place 2 anchovies on top of tomatoes. Dress rocket with lemon dressing and arrange on top of tart. Drizzle a little balsamic over and around.

Warm salad of prawns, southern golds, shaved fennel & chilli oil

Serves 6

4 baby fennel, outer leaves and core removed, finely shaved

1/2 red onion, finely sliced

1 cup picked coriander sprigs, washed and spun

1/2 cup (125ml/4 1/2 fl oz) mayonnaise (Basics page 156)

1 tablespoon seeded mustard (preferably Hill Farm Mountain Pepper)

grated zest of 1 lime

1 tablespoon (20ml) lime juice

12 medium southern gold (pink-eye) potatoes, steamed and peeled

olive oil

30 medium green prawns, peeled, butterflied with tails attached

salt/freshly ground black pepper

chilli oil (Basics page 157)

3 limes, halved

Toss fennel, onion and coriander in a bowl, reserving a few coriander sprigs.

Combine mayonnaise with mustard, lime zest and lime juice. Dress salad with mayonnaise to moisten.

Slice each potato in half. Heat a wide, heavy-based pan and fry potatoes cut side-down in a little olive oil until the surface has crisped and potatoes have good colour and are warmed through.

Season prawns and pan-fry, char-grill or barbecue until just cooked.

To serve, place 4 potato halves in the centre of each plate and top with 3 prawns. Arrange salad on top of prawns. Place remaining prawns on top. Drizzle a little chilli oil over and around. Top with reserved coriander and serve with lime halves.

Tartlet of caramelised onions, fetta & oven-roasted tomatoes

Serves 6

1 quantity savoury shortcrust pastry (Basics page 154)

olive oil

2 red onions, sliced

1 clove garlic, finely chopped

1 heaped tablespoon brown sugar

dash balsamic vinegar

salt/freshly ground black pepper

12 oven-roasted tomato halves (Basics page 167)

12 fresh basil leaves

200g (7 oz) fetta, diced

mixed salad leaves

lemon dressing (Basics page 160)

Prepare pastry as recipe directs. Roll out pastry and line six 8cm tart cases (preferably with removable bases). Blind bake, pricking the pastry rather than using weights (Basics page 155). Fully cook the cases & set aside.

Heat a little olive oil in a hot pan. Sweat onions with garlic until softened. Sprinkle in sugar and cook until onions caramelise. Add vinegar and season to taste.

Place onions on base of tart cases then layer with tomatoes, basil and fetta.

Warm tartlets in a moderate oven 180°C (350°F) for 5–10 minutes.

To serve, place a tartlet in the centre of each plate. Moisten salad leaves with lemon dressing and divide between the plates.

Right: Tartlet of caramelised onions, fetta & oven-roasted tomatoes

*Left: Seared cuttlefish & chorizo
sausage with salad of chickpeas,
tomatoes & chilli
(recipe page 78)*

*Right: Spinach & ricotta hotcakes,
smoked salmon, cucumber & radish
(recipe page 86)*

Steamed asparagus, fetta & wilted spinach with honey poppy seed dressing

Serves 6

30 asparagus spears, washed and trimmed

50g (2 oz) unsalted butter

salt/freshly ground black pepper

250g (9 oz) English spinach, washed and stems
   removed

1 red onion, finely sliced

250g (9 oz) fetta

6 lemon wedges, to serve

Dressing

2 tablespoons poppy seeds

90ml (3 oz) orange juice

2 teaspoons (10ml) Dijon mustard

90ml (3 fl oz) hazelnut oil

3 tablespoons (60ml/2 fl oz) honey

To make dressing, whisk all ingredients together in a bowl. Set aside.

Bring a large saucepan of salted water to the boil. Meanwhile, heat a large frying pan over medium heat.

Drop asparagus into boiling water and blanch until just tender. Remove asparagus with a slotted spoon and place in hot frying pan with butter and a little salt and pepper. Toss asparagus in butter and remove from pan. Keep warm.

Off the heat, add spinach and onion to the hot pan and toss until spinach begins to wilt. Return to heat briefly if necessary. Remove spinach from pan and transfer to a paper towel.

To serve, place 5 asparagus spears in the centre of each plate. Divide spinach between the plates, placing it on top of asparagus. Crumble fetta over spinach. Drizzle dressing over and around. Serve with lemon wedges.

Left: Steamed asparagus, fetta &
wilted spinach with honey poppy
seed dressing

Apple & rhubarb crumble with egg custard

Serves 6

Fresh egg custard should be kept warm once made. It is difficult to reheat, unless this is done carefully over a double boiler, stirring constantly.

500g (1 lb) caster sugar, approximately

250ml (9 oz) water

4 apples, peeled, cored and sliced

1 cinnamon stick

1 vanilla bean, split

2–3 whole cloves

10 stalks rhubarb, topped, tailed, outer string removed, cut diagonally

juice of 1 lemon

juice of 1 orange

extra sugar, optional

icing sugar, to serve

Crumble

300g (10½ oz) raw sugar

300g (10½ oz) shredded coconut

300g (10½ oz) digestive biscuits, crushed

200g (7 oz) almond meal

100g (3½ oz) plain flour

100g (3½ oz) rolled oats

pinch salt

250g (9 oz) softened unsalted butter, diced

To make filling, place sugar and water in a heavy-based saucepan and stir to combine. Cook over high heat until mixture begins to turn a light caramel. Add apples, cinnamon, vanilla and cloves and cook 2–3 minutes. Add rhubarb and continue cooking until both fruits have softened but still hold their shape. Stir through lemon and orange juice. Remove from heat and pour into a shallow flat tray to cool. If fruit is too acidic, adjust taste with extra sugar.

To make crumble, preheat oven to 180°C (350°F).

Place dry ingredients in a bowl. Using your hands, rub butter through dry ingredients until evenly distributed. Mixture should be rough in appearance.

Fill six 8–9cm (3–4 in) diameter x 4–5cm (1½–2 in) high ramekins or 1 large ovenproof dish with apple and rhubarb filling. Sprinkle crumble over top, approximately ½cm thick. Do not pack down, as this inhibits the crumble cooking properly.

Bake 15–20 minutes or until crumble is crisp and golden and filling is hot.

Continued opposite

Egg custard

1 vanilla bean, split
500ml (18 fl oz) pouring cream (35% butterfat)
6 egg yolks
150g (5 oz) caster sugar

To make custard, scrape seeds from vanilla bean into a saucepan, add cream and vanilla bean and heat almost to the boil. In a bowl, beat egg yolks with sugar until the mixture is light and pale. Pour hot cream, whisking continuously, then return to a clean saucepan. Cook over low heat, stirring continuously, until mixture thickens and coats the back of the wooden spoon. Do not boil.

Strain into a clean bowl. To avoid custard splitting, you may remove some of the excess heat by placing the bowl in a sink of iced water. Place plastic film directly on surface of custard to avoid a skin forming.

Dust crumbles with icing sugar and serve on underplates. Serve egg custard separately.

Apple, pecan & pine nut torte with apple gelati

Serves 10

This apple gelati fascinated customers at e'cco because it retained a bright green speck – achieved by freezing the apples with the skin on before puréeing them. It is a brilliant recipe that you must try!

6 Granny Smith apples, peeled, cored, quartered and sliced finely

grated zest and juice of 1 lemon

3 large eggs

250g (9 oz) caster sugar

2 teaspoons (10ml) vanilla essence

100g (3½ oz) unsalted butter, melted

100ml (3½ fl oz) milk

150g (5 oz) plain flour, sifted

2 teaspoons baking powder

100g (3½ oz) toasted pecans, ground

120g (4 oz) sultanas, chopped

100g (3½ oz) pine nuts, toasted

3 tablespoons (60g/2 oz) caster sugar, extra

1 teaspoon cinnamon

½ teaspoon nutmeg

icing sugar

Apple gelati

1kg (2 lb) Granny Smith apples, unpeeled, cored, quartered (approximately 6 apples)

juice of 1 lemon

500g (1 lb) caster sugar

500ml (18 fl oz) water

30ml (1 fl oz) Calvados (apple liqueur), optional

juice of 5 lemons, extra

To make torte, preheat oven to 160°C (325°F). Line the sides and base of a 26cm (10½ in) springform tin with non-stick baking (silicone) paper.

In a bowl, toss sliced apple with zest and juice of lemon to prevent browning. Set aside.

Place eggs, sugar and vanilla in a clean bowl and whisk until pale and creamy. Add butter and milk to egg mixture, combining well. Fold in flour and baking powder.

Place one-third of the pecans, sultanas, pine nuts, and apple on base of springform tin. Pour one-third of the cake batter over nuts and fruit. Repeat this process until all ingredients and cake batter have been used.

Combine extra sugar, cinnamon and nutmeg, and sprinkle over top of cake.

Bake approximately 1 hour 20 minutes, or until cooked when tested with a skewer. Cool on a cake rack.

To make gelati, toss apples in the juice of 1 lemon to prevent browning. Freeze apples in lemon juice.

In a heavy-based saucepan, dissolve sugar in water over medium heat to form a syrup. Chill.

In a blender, purée frozen apples with the extra lemon juice, sugar syrup and Calvados. Taste mixture; if too sweet, add more lemon juice to taste. Churn mixture in an ice cream machine and freeze.

To serve, place a generous slice of torte in the centre of each plate, dust with icing sugar and place 2 scoops of apple gelati alongside.

Apricot & Amaretto cake with caramel & cream

Serves 9

250g (9 oz) Australian dried apricots

250ml (9 fl oz) water

30ml (1 fl oz) Amaretto (almond liqueur)

6 eggs

225g (8 oz) caster sugar

225g (8 oz) almond meal

100g (3½ oz) plain flour

2 teaspoons baking powder

Caramel sauce

1 cup (250g/9 oz) caster sugar

½ cup (125ml/4½ fl oz) water

30ml (1 fl oz) Amaretto (almond liqueur)

apricot nectar

1 cup (250ml/9 fl oz) pure cream (45% butterfat such as King Island or Kirk's) to serve

Soak apricots in water and Amaretto overnight.

Preheat oven to 170–180°C (360–370°F). Line a 26cm (10 in) springform tin with non-stick baking (silicone) paper.

Pour apricots and soaking liquor into a small pan. Bring to the boil. Remove from heat and cool. Purée apricots and liquor in food processor until smooth.

Whisk eggs and sugar until light, fluffy and doubled in volume. Stir in almond meal, flour, baking powder and apricot purée.

Pour batter into prepared springform tin and bake for approximately 1 hour or until cooked when tested with a skewer.

To make caramel sauce, combine sugar and water in a heavy-based pan over moderate heat. Slowly bring to the boil, taking care that sugar is dissolved before it boils. Simmer until mixture turns a rich golden brown, then immediately remove from heat.

Taking great care as the caramel may spit, add Amaretto and a little apricot nectar to achieve a syrup consistency. Return saucepan to heat and stir until smooth, adding more apricot nectar if required.

To serve, place a wedge of cake in the centre of each plate. Place a spoonful of pure cream beside cake. Drizzle caramel sauce over and around cake.

Baked caramel pots with strawberries & honey madeleines

Serves 6

Madeleines can be made in advance and stored in an airtight container. They are best served warm.

225g (8 oz) caster sugar
¼ cup (60ml/2 fl oz) water
250ml (9 fl oz) milk
500ml (18 fl oz) pouring cream (35% butterfat)
7 egg yolks
2 punnets strawberries, washed and hulled
icing sugar

Honey madeleines

4 eggs
140g (5 oz) caster sugar
25g (1 oz) brown sugar
180g (6 oz) plain flour
2 teaspoons baking powder
180g (6 oz) unsalted butter, melted
2 tablespoons (40ml/1½ fl oz) honey

Preheat oven to 120°C (250°F).

To make caramel pots, gently heat sugar and water together in a saucepan, stirring until sugar dissolves. Bring to the boil and cook to a golden caramel.

Combine milk and cream in another saucepan and warm; do not boil. Add warm milk mixture to caramel, taking care as it may spit, and stir well to combine. Return to heat if necessary.

Beat egg yolks in a separate bowl until pale. Gradually whisk in hot caramel mixture. Strain.

Fill six 8–9cm (3 in) diameter x 4–5cm (2 in) high ramekins with caramel custard. Bake in a water bath for about 50 minutes or until custard is just set.

To make madeleines, preheat the oven to 160°C (325°F). Lightly grease madeleine moulds.

In an electric mixer, combine all ingredients. Fill madeleine moulds three-quarters full of mixture.

Bake approximately 9–10 minutes. Stand for 1 minute before turning out.

To serve, place caramel pots on an underplate. Serve with strawberries and warm madeleines dusted with icing sugar.

Bittersweet chocolate espresso cake with orange & Campari sorbet

Serves 9

This cake is best served warm or at room temperature.

400g (14 oz) dark (bittersweet, 55–70% cocoa mass) chocolate

300g (10¹/₂ oz) caster sugar

300g (10¹/₂ oz) unsalted butter

2 tablespoons instant espresso coffee dissolved in 3 tablespoons (40ml/1¹/₂ fl oz) hot water (or 2 short blacks)

2 tablespoons (40ml/1¹/₂ fl oz) dark rum (preferably Bundaberg)

200g (7 oz) ground almonds

10 eggs, separated

Orange & Campari sorbet

350ml (12 fl oz) water

350g (12 oz) caster sugar

600ml (1 pint) orange or blood orange juice

Campari to taste

juice of 4–5 lemons

Preheat oven to 180°C (350°F). Grease a 26cm (10 in) springform tin and line with non-stick baking (silicone) paper.

Melt chocolate, sugar, butter, coffee and rum in a double saucepan. Transfer mixture to a bowl and stir in ground almonds. Beat in egg yolks one at a time.

Whisk egg whites until they form firm peaks. Gently fold half the whites into chocolate coffee mixture then fold in the remaining half.

Pour batter into the springform tin and bake 20 minutes. Turn the oven down to 160°C (325°F). Cover cake with aluminium foil to prevent it burning on the outside, and cook for a further 1 hour. Test cake by inserting a fine skewer into the centre – it should come out clean.

Remove cake from oven and cool in tin on a cake rack. Cover cake with a damp cloth so that the 'crust' remains moist.

To make sorbet, place water and sugar in a saucepan and bring to the boil, ensuring the sugar is dissolved. Remove from the heat, allow to cool, then refrigerate until completely chilled before using. At this stage you should have 500ml (18 fl oz) of sugar syrup.

Mix together sugar syrup, orange juice and Campari. Taste for sweetness and adjust with lemon juice.

Churn mixture in an ice cream maker. Store in freezer.

Serve wedges of cake dusted with icing sugar and a generous scoop of sorbet.

Buttermilk pancakes with caramelised pear & honeycomb ice cream

Serves 10

Honeycomb can be quite cantankerous. If you do have a failure, discard it and try again because it is worth the effort for this ice cream.

vanilla bean ice cream (Basics page 171)
caramel sauce (Basics page 176)
clarified butter, melted (Basics page 155)

Honeycomb

250g (9 oz) caster sugar
100g (3¹/₂ oz) glucose
2 tablespoons (40ml/1¹/₂ fl oz) water
³/₄ teaspoon bicarbonate of soda

Pancakes

250g (9 oz) plain flour
pinch salt
1 tablespoon baking powder
1 teaspoon bicarbonate of soda
100g (3¹/₂ oz) caster sugar
500ml (18 fl oz) buttermilk
4 eggs, separated

Pears

125g (4¹/₂ oz) unsalted butter
300g (10¹/₂ oz) caster sugar
8 pears, peeled, cored and sliced lengthways

Prepare vanilla bean ice cream, caramel sauce and clarified butter as recipes direct.

To make honeycomb, line a baking tray with non-stick baking (silicone) paper and set aside.

In a saucepan, place sugar, glucose and water and heat gently until sugar dissolves. Heat for 10 minutes or until temperature reads 154°C on a sugar thermometer ("hard crack"). Quickly stir in bicarbonate of soda.

Pour honeycomb into prepared baking tray and leave to cool. When honeycomb is completely cold, crack into pieces using a rolling pin or the back of a metal spoon. Fold honeycomb through ice cream when it is nearly churned. Freeze.

To make pancakes, sift flour, salt, baking powder and bicarbonate of soda into a large bowl. Stir in sugar. Whisk together buttermilk and egg yolks. Make a well in centre of dry ingredients and add buttermilk mixture. Mix well together. Whisk egg whites until firm peaks form. Gently fold through pancake mixture in 2 batches.

Heat blini pans over moderate heat and brush with clarified butter. Fill blini pans three-quarters full with pancake mixture. Once bubbles appear, carefully turn pancakes using a spatula or palette knife. Continue to cook until set. Turn pancakes out onto cake rack. Keep warm.

To cook pears, place butter and sugar into a large saucepan and cook until golden. Add pears and cook until tender, coating well in caramel. Set aside.

To serve, place a pancake in the centre of a serving plate. Top with slices of caramelised pear and scoop some honeycomb ice cream on top. Serve drizzled with caramel sauce.

Caramelised rum bananas with toasted banana bread

Serves 6

1½ cups (190g/6 oz) self-raising flour

½ teaspoon bicarbonate of soda

pinch nutmeg

pinch salt

¾ cup (150g/5 oz) raw sugar

125g (4 oz) unsalted butter, melted

2 eggs, lightly beaten

½ (2.5ml) teaspoon vanilla essence

¼ cup (60ml/2 fl oz) milk

3 large ripe bananas, mashed

6 cavendish bananas, extra, peeled and sliced
diagonally into 3 strips

1 cup (250ml/9 fl oz) pure cream (45% butterfat such
as King Island or Kirk's), to serve

Rum caramel

375g (13 oz) caster sugar

water

120ml (4 fl oz) dark rum (preferably Bundaberg)

100ml (3½ fl oz) pouring cream (35% butterfat)

Preheat oven to 160°C (325°F).

Grease a loaf tin approximately 30cm (12 in) long x 10cm (4 in) wide x 8cm (3 in) high and line with non-stick baking (silicone) paper.

Sift flour, bicarbonate of soda, nutmeg and salt into a bowl. Stir in sugar.

In a separate bowl, combine melted butter, eggs, vanilla, milk and mashed bananas. Fold mixture into dry ingredients.

Pour mixture into the loaf tin and bake 45–50 minutes or until a skewer inserted comes out clean and loaf springs back when touched.

Leave in tin for 5 minutes before turning onto a cake rack.

To make rum caramel, place sugar in a large, clean, flat frying pan and add enough water to dissolve. Bring to the boil without stirring until it begins to turn a dark caramel.

Add banana slices and toss lightly. Remove from heat and add rum. Return to heat and continue to cook until bananas begin to soften.

Using a slotted spoon, remove bananas and set aside. Place pan back on heat, add cream and bring back to the boil briefly. Strain caramel.

Cut 6 large slices of banana bread (the loaf makes 9–10). Toast lightly under grill or in toaster.

To serve, cut each slice of banana bread in half and lay diagonally on each plate. Divide bananas on top of each portion of bread. Drizzle caramel over and around and serve with a generous spoonful of pure cream to one side.

Cherry frangipane

Serves 9

Frangipane is best served at room temperature on the day it is made.

sweet shortcrust pastry (Basics page 154)

250g (9 oz) unsalted butter

250g (9 oz) caster sugar

4 eggs

60g (2 oz) plain flour, sifted

250g (9 oz) almond meal

2 cups fresh cherries, pitted and stems removed

icing sugar

1 cup (250ml/9 fl oz) pure cream (45% butterfat such as King Island or Kirk's)

grated zest of 1 lime

12 cherries, extra

Prepare shortcrust pastry as recipe directs. Line a 24cm (9¹/₂ in) removable-base tart tin with pastry and blind bake (Basics page 155) as recipe directs .

Reduce oven temperature to 150°C (300°F).

To make frangipane, cream butter and sugar together until light and fluffy. Beat in eggs, one at a time. Combine flour and almond meal in a separate bowl. Fold through butter mixture.

Place pitted cherries in base of prepared pastry shell. Spoon in frangipane and smooth out top with the back of a hot metal spoon. Bake 40–50 minutes or until set.

To serve, cut a wedge of frangipane tart and dust with icing sugar. Place in the centre of a plate. Serve with a spoonful of pure cream. Garnish with a little lime zest over cream and extra cherries.

Chocolate sour cream cake

Serves 10–12

This is one of the easiest and most successful cakes you'll come across. The recipe came from Pamela Lawson, who runs the brilliant Pamela's Pantry in Paddington, Brisbane, which has supplied Brisbane for over 20 years with high-quality home-cooked food.

1 cup (250ml/9 fl oz) water

2 cups (250g/9 oz) plain flour, sifted

2 cups (400g/14 oz) caster sugar

2 whole eggs

$1/2$ teaspoon baking powder

$1^1/_4$ teaspoons bicarbonate of soda

3 tablespoons (30g/1 oz) cocoa

$3/_4$ cup ($6^1/_2$ oz) sour cream

80g (3 oz) unsalted butter, at room temperature

$1/_2$ teaspoon salt

Preheat oven to 160°C (325°F). Grease a 24cm ($9^1/_2$ in) springform tin and line base with non-stick baking (silicone) paper.

Place all ingredients in an electric mixer and combine on slow speed for 2 minutes. Scrape down sides and mix at full speed for a further 2 minutes.

Pour mixture into the springform tin. Bake 50–60 minutes or until a fine skewer inserted into the centre of cake comes out clean.

Cool cake in pan for 10 minutes before turning out onto a cake rack to cool completely.

Note: This cake is delicious served in a variety of ways: with pouring cream and fresh berries; icing the top with chocolate ganache or your favourite chocolate icing; or simply dust with icing sugar and serve with orange confit (Basics page 173).

Chocolate truffle cake & Grand Marnier sorbet

Serves 9

Remove cake from refrigerator 30–40 minutes prior to serving to allow chocolate truffle to soften slightly. It should have a soft velvety texture once cut. If this is not the case, allow to stand at room temperature for several more minutes.

chocolate sour cream cake (page 109)

warm raspberry jam

cocoa, for dusting

Grand Marnier sorbet (Basics page 172), to serve

Truffle

110ml (4 fl oz) pouring cream (35% butterfat)

110g (4 oz) unsalted butter, cubed

230g (8 oz) dark couverture chocolate, grated

2¹/₂ leaves gelatine, soaked in cold water and squeezed out

30ml (1 fl oz) dark rum (preferably Bundaberg)

400ml (14 fl oz) pouring cream (35% butterfat), whipped softly

Prepare Grand Marnier sorbet as recipe directs.

Preheat oven to 165°C (330°F). Grease a 26cm (10¹/₂ in) springform tin and line base with non-stick baking (silicone) paper.

Prepare chocolate sour cream cake as recipe directs.

Clean and re-line the base and sides of the springform tin.

Using a long, serrated knife, thinly slice cake horizontally to obtain a 1cm (¹/₂ in) thick disc. Place this in the base of springform tin. Brush over enough raspberry jam to moisten cake. (The remaining cake may be kept in the refrigerator for several days, or frozen for another use).

To make truffle, place cream and butter in a saucepan and bring to the boil. Place chocolate in a bowl and pour cream and butter mixture over chocolate. Stir to combine. Add gelatine and continue to stir until completely dissolved. Fold in rum. Once chocolate is at room temperature, carefully fold in whipped cream and immediately pour into prepared tin. Smooth top using back of a warm serving spoon. Refrigerate overnight or until set.

To serve, using a hot knife, cut a wedge of cake and place in the centre of plate. Dust top with cocoa and serve with Grand Marnier sorbet.

Coconut tart with pineapple, mint & crème fraîche

Serves 9

This dessert was a great success at the Sounds of Silence dinners where e'cco's food was featured during April 2000. The Sounds of Silence experience is run most of the year by Ayers Rock Resort (weather permitting). The guests dine at dusk, in a truly amazing setting under the stars, with Uluru and Kata Tjuta (formerly The Olgas) as a backdrop.

sweet shortcrust pastry (Basics page 154)

icing sugar, to serve

1 cup (250g/ 9 oz) crème fraîche

1 cup (250g/9 oz) pineapple, diced

¼ cup mint leaves, roughly chopped

juice of 1 lime

Filling

3 eggs

grated zest of 2 lemons

200g (7 oz) caster sugar

400ml (14 fl oz) thickened cream

juice of 2 lemons

30ml (1 oz) Malibu (coconut liqueur)

250g (9 oz) desiccated coconut

Prepare shortcrust pastry as recipe directs. Line a 24cm (9½ in) removable-base tart tin with prepared shortcrust pastry and blind bake as recipe directs.

To make filling, reduce oven temperature to 120°C (250°F).

Beat eggs, lemon zest and caster sugar for 1 minute. Gently fold in cream, then add lemon juice and Malibu. Lastly add coconut.

Pour mixture into pastry shell and bake until golden, approximately 40–50 minutes.

Combine pineapple, mint and lime juice in a bowl.

To serve, cut tart into 9 portions. Dust top with icing sugar. Place a wedge of tart on each plate. Place a spoonful of crème fraîche next to tart. Spoon pineapple mixture onto crème fraîche.

Fresh passionfruit can be spooned over the crème fraîche instead of pineapple and mint for a variation.

Caramelised peaches, peach ice cream & glass biscuits

Serves 6

Peach purée

6 large or 9 medium very ripe peaches, washed
juice of half a lemon

Peach ice cream

300g (10½ oz) caster sugar
12 egg yolks
700ml (1¼ pints) pouring cream (35% butterfat)
300ml (10½ fl oz) strained peach purée (above)
60ml (2 oz) peach liqueur
juice of 2–3 lemons, to taste

glass biscuits (Basics page 173), to serve

Caramelised peaches

¾ cup (6½ oz) caster sugar
water
6 large or 9 medium ripe but firm freestone peaches, quartered
60ml (2 fl oz) peach liqueur
juice of ½ lemon
good knob unsalted butter (optional)

To make peach purée, cut peach flesh away from stone and place in food processor with lemon juice. Blend until smooth. Pass through a fine sieve.

To make ice cream, in a bowl, whisk together sugar and egg yolks until well combined.

In a 2 litre (3½ pint) saucepan, bring cream almost to the boil. Whisk hot cream mixture into eggs and sugar, then return mixture to clean saucepan over low heat.

Using a wooden spoon, stir constantly until custard thickens and coats the back of the spoon. Do not let mixture boil. Strain through a fine sieve and refrigerate until cold.

Add purée and liqueur to chilled ice cream base and adjust flavour with lemon juice. Churn in an ice cream machine.

Prepare glass biscuits as recipe directs.

To make caramelised peaches, place sugar in a heavy-based saucepan with enough water to dissolve sugar. Cook over high heat until mixture just begins to turn to a light caramel colour. Add peach wedges and continue to cook until they begin to soften. During cooking, add more water if necessary to maintain the consistency of the syrup. Remove from heat and gently stir in liqueur, lemon juice and butter.

To serve, place peaches in the base of wide soup bowls. Top with a glass biscuit and a generous scoop of peach ice cream.

Right: Caramelised peaches, peach ice cream & glass biscuits

*Left: Apple, pecan & pine nut torte
with apple gelati
(recipe page 102)*

*Right: Baked caramel pots with
strawberries & honey madeleines
(recipe page 104)*

*Left: Caramelised rum bananas with
toasted banana bread
(recipe page 107)*

*Right: Coconut tart with pineapple,
mint & crème fraîche
(recipe page 111)*

Chocolate, whisky & raisin cake with soft cream

Serves 9

$^1/_2$ cup raisins
250ml (9 fl oz) whisky
220g (8 oz) unsalted butter
1$^1/_2$ cups (375g/13 oz) caster sugar
6 eggs, separated
440g (15$^1/_2$ oz) dark chocolate, melted
140g (5 oz) plain flour, sifted
pinch salt
1$^1/_2$ cups (375g/13 oz) ground almonds
125ml (4$^1/_2$ fl oz) milk

Soft cream

375ml (13 fl oz) pouring cream (35% butterfat)
1 tablespoon (20g) caster sugar
1 teaspoon vanilla essence

Raisins in whisky syrup

$^1/_2$ cup (125g/4$^1/_2$ oz) brown sugar
125ml (4$^1/_2$ fl oz) water
45ml (1$^1/_2$ fl oz) whisky
1 cup raisins

Soak raisins in whisky, preferably overnight.

To make cake, preheat oven to 190°C (375°F). Line the sides and base of a 20–24cm (8–9$^1/_2$ in) cake tin with non-stick baking (silicone) paper.

Cream butter and sugar until light and fluffy. Add egg yolks one by one, combining well after each addition. Stir in chocolate, then fold in flour, salt, almonds, milk, raisins and whisky.

In a clean dry bowl, whisk egg whites until they form stiff peaks. Gently fold whites into chocolate mixture one-third at a time.

Pour mixture into prepared cake tin and bake for 1 hour, then turn down heat to 160°C (325°F) and bake for a further 20 minutes or until cooked through (a skewer will come out clean). Leave to cool on a cake rack.

To make soft cream, combine cream, sugar and vanilla in a bowl. Whip until firm and refrigerate until required.

To make raisins in whisky syrup, in a small saucepan bring sugar and water to the boil, stirring occasionally, to form a syrup. Remove from the heat then add whisky and raisins to hot syrup. Leave to cool. If syrup begins to crystallise, warm slightly just before serving.

To serve, place a warm slice of cake in the centre of each plate. Top with a generous spoonful of soft cream. Spoon some of the raisins over cream and drizzle with whisky syrup.

Left: Chocolate, whisky & raisin cake with soft cream

Espresso cheesecake with Kahlua muscatels

Serves 9

250g (9 oz) muscatels (dried grapes on stems)
Kahlua (coffee liqueur), to cover
sweet shortcrust pastry (Basics page 154)

Filling

675g (1¹/₃ lb) cream cheese (Philadelphia), not light
2 eggs
3 tablespoons (30g/1 oz) cornflour
1 teaspoon vanilla essence
225g (8 oz) caster sugar
3 tablespoons (15g/¹/₂ oz) instant espresso coffee
2 tablespoons (40ml/1¹/₂ fl oz) pouring cream (35% butterfat), warm
250ml (9 fl oz) pouring cream (35% butterfat), lightly whipped

Soak muscatels in Kahlua overnight.

Make sweet shortcrust pastry as recipe directs.

Roll a large circle of pastry, 26–28cm (11 in) in diameter (allowing for shrinkage) on a baking tray lined with non-stick baking (silicone) paper. Bake at 160°C (325°F) for approximately 30 minutes, or until cooked and starting to colour.

Press a 24cm (9¹/₂ in) cake ring onto cooked pastry to form a flat base. Discard excess pastry.

Reduce oven temperature to 120°C (250°F).

To make the filling, in a food processor, blend cream cheese until smooth. Add eggs, one at a time, then cornflour, vanilla and sugar. Dissolve coffee in warm cream and mix into cream cheese mixture. Remove from processor and transfer to a bowl. Using a whisk, fold in lightly whipped cream.

Pour filling into the cake ring on top of pastry and bake 20–25 minutes. Filling will change colour slightly but will not be completely set. Remove from oven and cool. Refrigerate until firm.

To serve, place a wedge of cheesecake in the centre of each serving plate. Drain muscatels and reserve liquid. Arrange a pile of muscatels alongside then drizzle reserved liquid over and around cheesecake.

Frangipane tart, raspberries & honey Champagne cream

Serves 9

I first came across this cream while working in London in 1984 at Antony Worrall Thompson's restaurant Mènage à Trois, where it was served over poached peaches, and I have probably used this cream in one way or another every summer since.

sweet shortcrust pastry (Basics page 154)

icing sugar for dusting

2 punnets raspberries

frangipane (Basics page 174)

Honey Champagne cream

250ml (9 fl oz) pouring cream (35% butterfat)

1 tablespoon (20ml) honey

1 teaspoon lemon juice

Champagne

sugar syrup (Basics page 176)

Prepare sweet shortcrust pastry as recipe directs. Line a 24cm (9½ in) removable-base tart tin with prepared pastry and blind bake (Basics page 155).

Prepare frangipane as recipe directs.

Prepare sugar syrup as recipe directs.

To make honey Champagne cream, whip cream, honey and lemon juice until soft peaks form. Add a little Champagne and balance flavour with sugar syrup. The cream will thicken while standing in refrigerator and can be thinned with either more Champagne, sugar syrup, orange juice or peach juice.

To serve, cut a wedge of tart and dust with icing sugar. Place in the centre of a plate. Place a generous spoonful of honey Champagne cream over tart. Scatter raspberries onto cream and around plate.

Frozen bittersweet chocolate parfait with chocolate biscotti

Serves 6–8

The parfait will go very firm in the freezer, so make sure you cut your portions and allow to sit on the individual plates for several minutes prior to serving.

1/2 cup sultanas, roughly chopped

60ml (2 oz) boiling water

60ml (2 oz) Crème de Cacao (chocolate liqueur)

icing sugar

Parfait

2 eggs

2 egg yolks, extra

125g (4 1/2 oz) caster sugar

225g (8 oz) dark chocolate (bittersweet 55–70% cocoa mass), melted

1 tablespoon (20ml) Cointreau (orange liqueur)

1 teaspoon vanilla essence

350ml (12 oz) pouring cream (35% butterfat), whipped to soft peaks

Chocolate biscotti

215g (7 1/2 oz) plain flour

3 tablespoons (60g/2 oz) good-quality Dutch cocoa powder

1/4 teaspoon baking powder

pinch salt

250g (9 oz) caster sugar

2 eggs, beaten

1/2 teaspoon grated orange zest

1/4 teaspoon vanilla essence

175g (6 oz) whole almonds, skin on

To make the parfait, whisk together eggs, extra yolks and sugar until mixture is pale and thick. Stir in melted chocolate. Add Cointreau and vanilla. Combine well. Make sure mixture is not too hot before gently folding in cream.

Line a Le Creuset (or similar) loaf tin approximately 30cm (12 in) length x 10cm (4 in) wide x 8cm (3 in) high with plastic wrap, allowing 3–4 cm (1–1 1/2 in) overhang. Pour parfait into lined loaf tin, tap lightly on work surface to remove air bubbles. Cover top gently with overhanging plastic wrap and freeze overnight until set.

To make biscotti, preheat oven to 180°C (350°F). Sift flour, cocoa, baking powder and salt into a bowl. Stir in sugar. Make a well in the centre and add eggs, orange zest and vanilla. Gently mix to combine, then stir in almonds.

On a floured surface, press mixture into a well formed rectangular shape (to ensure it holds) and place on an oven tray lined with non-stick baking (silicone) paper. Bake for 45 minutes or until firm. Remove from oven and cool completely.

Cut biscotti shape into very thin slices, approximately 2–3mm thick, and lay slices flat on oven trays. Return to very cool electric oven, approximately 80°C (125°F), to dry biscotti until crisp. Biscotti can also be dried overnight in a gas oven with just the pilot light on.

Place sultanas in a bowl and add boiling water and Crème de Cacao. Allow to infuse. Once cool, store in an airtight container in the refrigerator.

To serve, cut parfait into slices approximately 1 1/2 cm (1/2 in) thick. Place a slice in centre of each plate. Spoon sultanas over and around parfait. Serve with chocolate biscotti dusted with icing sugar.

Grilled pineapple, gingerbread & toasted coconut ice cream

Serves 6

6 slices pineapple, approximately 1$\frac{1}{2}$cm ($\frac{1}{2}$ in) thick, core removed

caster sugar

toasted coconut ice cream (Basics page 171)

gingerbread (Basics page 175)

Caramel

250g (9 oz) caster sugar

125ml (4$\frac{1}{2}$ fl oz) water

60ml (2 oz) Malibu (coconut liqueur)

Prepare gingerbread as recipe directs.

Prepare toasted coconut ice cream as recipe directs.

To make caramel, combine sugar and water in a small saucepan over moderate heat and stir until sugar dissolves. Bring to the boil and boil until syrup turns a golden colour. Remove from heat immediately. Carefully, as mixture may spit, add Malibu. Return saucepan to heat and stir until syrup is smooth and returns to the boil. Strain syrup and cool.

To grill pineapple, preheat grill to moderate. Place pineapple on a non-stick tray and sprinkle liberally with sugar. Place under grill until pineapple is tender and light golden in colour.

To serve, place a slice of pineapple in the base of each soup bowl. Top with a slice of gingerbread (at room temperature or gently warmed under grill). Drizzle liberally with caramel and serve with 1 or 2 scoops of toasted coconut ice cream.

Hazelnut & chocolate torte with Frangelico cream

Serves 9

Meringue

8 egg whites
pinch salt
300g (10$\frac{1}{2}$ oz) caster sugar
1 tablespoon (20g) cornflour
2 heaped tablespoons (40g/1$\frac{1}{2}$ oz) cocoa powder
2 teaspoons (10ml) vanilla essence

Chocolate ganache

400g (14 oz) good-quality cooking chocolate
250ml (9 fl oz) pouring cream (35% butterfat)
45ml (1$\frac{1}{2}$ fl oz) dark rum (preferably Bundaberg)

Frangelico cream

1 cup (250ml/9 fl oz) pouring cream (35% butterfat)
2 tablespoons icing sugar
2 tablespoons (40ml/1$\frac{1}{2}$ fl oz) Frangelico (hazelnut liqueur)

1 cup (9 oz) hazelnuts, roasted, skinned and roughly chopped
cocoa for dusting

To make meringue, preheat oven to 160°C (325°F). Line 3 baking trays with non-stick baking (silicone) paper. Draw a circle approximately 24cm (9$\frac{1}{2}$ in) in diameter on each piece of baking paper.

In an electric mixer, whisk egg whites with salt until frothy. Add caster sugar gradually, beating continuously, until egg whites form stiff peaks. Sift cornflour and cocoa together and fold into meringue mixture. Stir in vanilla.

Using a spatula, divide meringue between the 3 baking trays. Form into circles approximately 1$\frac{1}{2}$–2cm ($\frac{3}{4}$ in) high. Smooth out tops.

Bake 1–1$\frac{1}{2}$ hours until dry and crisp and some colour is achieved.

To make ganache, grate chocolate into a bowl. In a saucepan, bring cream to the boil. Pour cream over chocolate and stir until chocolate has melted. Stir in rum. Cool to room temperature.

To assemble torte, remove meringues from baking paper. Spread half the ganache onto one meringue disc. Sprinkle half the hazelnuts onto ganache. Place second meringue disc on top. Repeat process, finishing with a meringue disc.

To make Frangelico cream, whip cream with icing sugar until it forms soft peaks. Fold in Frangelico.

To serve, cut a wedge of torte using a serrated knife and place in centre of a plate. Dust top with cocoa. Serve with a generous spoonful of Frangelico cream.

Honey roasted pears with warm gingerbread & Greek yoghurt

Serves 6

gingerbread (Basics page 175)

4 beurre bosc pears, cored and halved
light olive oil
icing sugar
1 cup (250ml/9 fl oz) Greek-style yoghurt
honey

Prepare gingerbread as recipe directs.

To roast pears, preheat oven to 200°C (400°F).

Slice pear halves into 3 equal wedges. Heat a non-stick ovenproof pan over medium heat. Toss pears with a little oil until they begin to colour. Place pan in oven for 5–10 minutes, or until pears are tender.

To serve, place a warm slice of gingerbread in the centre of each plate. Dust with icing sugar and place 4 pear wedges alongside. Serve with a spoonful of yoghurt. Drizzle honey over pears.

Lemon pudding with blueberries & lemon butter

Serves 8

160g (5½ oz) unsalted butter, softened

350g (12 oz) caster sugar

8 eggs, separated

grated zest of 3 lemons

500ml (18 fl oz) milk

100g (3½ oz) plain flour, sifted

6 tablespoons (120ml/4 fl oz) lemon juice

icing sugar

lemon butter (Basics page 172)

2 punnets fresh blueberries, washed

To make pudding, preheat oven to 170°C (340°F). Lightly grease eight ramekins, 9cm (3½ in) diameter x 4–5cm (2 in) high.

Cream butter and sugar until light and pale. Add egg yolks one at a time, mixing well in between, then stir in lemon zest.

Using a whisk, add milk alternately with flour, combining well after each addition. Lastly, fold in lemon juice.

In a clean, dry bowl, whisk egg whites until stiff peaks form. Briskly fold one-third of the egg whites into lemon mixture. Gently fold in remaining egg whites.

Fill ramekins about three-quarters full with lemon mixture. Place in an ovenproof dish. Pour in boiling water to come halfway up the ramekins. Cover with aluminium foil. Bake until mixture is set, 25–30 minutes. The tops should be firm to the touch.

Prepare lemon butter as recipe directs.

To serve, remove ramekins from water bath and place on underplate. Dust with icing sugar and serve with lemon butter and blueberries.

White chocolate & lemon cheesecake

Serves 9

sweet shortcrust pastry (Basics page 154)
white chocolate shavings
glazed fruit

Cheesecake

500g (1 lb) cream cheese (Philadelphia), not light
2 eggs
grated zest of 2 lemons
225g (8 oz) caster sugar
1 teaspoon (5ml) vanilla essence
3 tablespoons (30g/1 oz) cornflour
400g (14 oz) white chocolate, melted
300ml (10^1/$_2$ fl oz) pouring cream (35% butterfat)

Lemon sauce

juice of 3–4 lemons
caster sugar to taste
grated zest of 2 lemons

Make sweet shortcrust pastry as recipe directs.

Preheat oven to 160°C (325°F).

Roll a large circle of pastry, 26–28cm (11 in) in diameter (allowing for shrinkage) on a baking tray lined with non-stick baking (silicone) paper. Bake approximately 30 minutes, or until cooked and starting to colour.

Press a 24cm (9^1/$_2$ in) cake ring onto cooked pastry to form a flat base. Discard excess pastry.

To make cheesecake, reduce oven temperature to 120°C (250°F).

Beat cream cheese until soft. In a separate bowl, mix together eggs, lemon zest, sugar, vanilla and cornflour. Add to cream cheese and continue beating. Add melted chocolate and cream. Continue beating until well combined.

Pour filling into the cake ring on top of the pastry and bake for 20–25 minutes. Filling will change colour slightly but will not be completely set. Remove from oven and cool. Refrigerate until firm.

To make lemon sauce, place all ingredients into a pan and heat gently until sugar dissolves. Reduce by one-third. Strain and set aside to cool.

Serve sliced cheesecake with shavings of white chocolate, glazed fruit and lemon sauce.

Macadamia tart with vanilla cream

Serves 9

sweet shortcrust pastry (Basics page 154)

Filling

1/2 cup (125ml/4 1/2 fl oz) golden syrup

1 cup (200g/7 oz) brown sugar

1 teaspoon mixed spice

1/2 cup (125ml/4 1/2 fl oz) pouring cream (35% butterfat)

120g (4 oz) unsalted butter, melted

6 eggs, beaten

2 cups (250g/9 oz) roughly chopped macadamia nuts

Vanilla cream

1 vanilla bean

1 cup (250ml/9 fl oz) pouring cream (35% butterfat)

2 tablespoons (40g/1 1/2 oz) caster sugar

Preheat oven to 180°C (350°F).

Prepare pastry as recipe directs. Roll out and line a 24cm (9 1/2 in) removable-base tart tin. Blind bake pastry case (Basics page 155) as recipe directs.

To make filling, reduce oven to 160°C (325°F). Combine all ingredients except macadamias in a large bowl. Lastly, fold in macadamias.

Pour mixture into cooled tart case and bake 40 minutes or until set. Leave to cool completely in the pan.

To make vanilla cream, scrape vanilla bean into cream. Whip cream until it forms soft peaks, adding sugar to taste. Chill until required.

To serve, slice tart into wedges. Place a wedge on the centre of each plate and place a spoonful of cream on the side.

Red wine pear pudding & pure cream

Serves 6

This recipe is also successful with pears poached in sugar syrup. Simply replace the red wine with water – but the pears won't have the pale red colour.

Red wine poached pears

1 litre (1½ pints) good-quality red wine

750g (1½ lb) caster sugar

1 bay leaf

2 cloves

1 cinnamon stick

grated zest of 1 orange

1 star anise

1 teaspoon cracked black peppercorns

3 beurre bosc pears, peeled, halved and cored

Butter sauce

125g (4½ oz) unsalted butter

250ml (9 fl oz) milk

150g (5 oz) caster sugar

Pudding

80g (3 oz) unsalted butter

220g (8 oz) caster sugar

2 eggs

185g (6½ oz) plain flour

2 teaspoons baking powder

¼ teaspoon salt

1 cup (9 fl oz) milk

reserved poaching liquor

1 cup (250ml/9 oz) pure cream (45% butterfat such as King Island or Kirk's)

To poach pears, combine all ingredients except pears in a large saucepan. Bring to the boil, immerse pears and cover with non-stick baking (silicone) paper and a plate to keep pears completely submerged during poaching. Poach gently until tender. Cool pears in poaching liquor.

Remove pears and set aside. Reduce poaching liquor to syrup consistency and reserve.

To make butter sauce, combine all ingredients in a saucepan and bring to the boil. Simmer for 2 minutes. Set aside.

To make pudding, preheat oven to 160°C (325°F). Lightly grease and flour six 15cm (6 in) fluted tartlet moulds.

Cream butter and sugar together until light and pale. Beat in eggs one at a time. In a bowl, sift together flour, baking powder and salt. Fold through half the dry ingredients then half the milk. Fold through remaining dry ingredients and remaining milk.

Spoon 2 tablespoons of batter into each mould, then add half a poached pear, cut-side down. Fill moulds around pears with remaining batter to approximately three-quarters full and bake 15–20 minutes or until cooked.

To serve, remove puddings from moulds and place a pudding in the middle of each plate. Using a pastry brush, liberally moisten top of puddings with butter sauce to soak in. Drizzle a little reduced poaching liquor over and around puddings. Serve with pure cream.

Malted milk parfait with hazelnut crisps and butterscotch sauce

Serves 12

6 egg yolks

140g (5 oz) caster sugar

4 tablespoons (80ml/3 fl oz) water

450ml (15$\frac{1}{2}$ fl oz) pouring cream (35% butterfat)

60ml (2 fl oz) Armagnac or Cognac

10 tablespoons (100g/3$\frac{1}{2}$ oz) malted milk powder

1–2 tablespoons (20–40ml) honey, to taste

pinch freshly grated nutmeg, to taste

hazelnut crisps (Basics page 174)

icing sugar, for dusting

Butterscotch sauce

225g (8 oz) caster sugar

100ml (3$\frac{1}{2}$ fl oz) water

300ml (10$\frac{1}{2}$ fl oz) pouring cream (35% butterfat)

125g (4$\frac{1}{2}$ oz) unsalted butter, cut into cubes

To make parfait, line a 21cm (8$\frac{1}{2}$ in) x 11cm (4$\frac{1}{2}$ in) loaf tin with plastic wrap allowing 3–4cm (1–1$\frac{1}{2}$ in) overhang.

Whisk egg yolks until pale and fluffy. In a saucepan, heat sugar and water to soft ball stage, 112°C (233°F) on a sugar thermometer. Gradually drizzle syrup into egg yolks, whisking constantly, until combined. Cool mixture to room temperature.

Whip cream until soft peaks form, then gradually fold in Armagnac, malted milk, honey and nutmeg to taste. Fold cream mixture into egg yolks.

Pour parfait into prepared tin and freeze overnight.

To make butterscotch sauce, place sugar and water into a saucepan and bring to the boil, ensuring sugar is completely dissolved. Cook until mixture becomes a dark caramel, being careful not to burn it.

Add cream with care, as caramel may spit. Bring back to the boil. Remove from heat and whisk in butter until melted and caramel is smooth. Strain and set aside to cool.

Make hazelnut crisps as recipe directs.

To serve, cut slices of parfait approximately 1$\frac{1}{2}$cm ($\frac{1}{2}$ in) thick with a hot knife. Place in the centre of a plate and drizzle with butterscotch sauce. Dust hazelnut crisp with icing sugar and rest against parfait.

Citrus sauternes cake with mango & Cointreau cream

Serves 8–10

3 mangoes, skinned and sliced

Citrus sauternes cake

6 eggs, separated
100g (3½ oz) caster sugar
2 teaspoons grated lemon zest
2 teaspoons grated orange zest
130ml (4½ fl oz) extra-virgin olive oil
100ml (3½ fl oz) sauternes
2 tablespoons (40ml/1½ fl oz) lemon juice
2 tablespoons (40ml/1½ fl oz) orange juice
160g (5½ oz) plain flour
pinch salt
½ teaspoon cream of tartar
100g (3½ oz) caster sugar, extra

Orange syrup

200g (7 oz) caster sugar
100ml (3½ fl oz) water
grated zest of 3 oranges
juice of 1–2 oranges, to taste

Cointreau cream

1 cup (250ml/9 fl oz) pouring cream (35% butterfat)
2 tablespoons (40g/1½ oz) caster sugar
grated zest of 1 orange
30ml (1 oz) Cointreau (orange liqueur)

To make the cake, preheat oven to 170°C (360°F). Grease and line the base of a 28–30cm (11–12 in) diameter x 3–4cm (1–1½ in) high quiche dish with non-stick baking (silicone) paper.

Whisk egg yolks with sugar. Add lemon and orange zest then whisk in olive oil, sauternes, lemon juice and orange juice.

Sift flour with salt and gently fold into egg yolk mixture until just combined.

Whisk egg whites with cream of tartar to form soft peaks, then slowly whisk in extra sugar until stiff peaks form. Gently fold whites into sauternes mixture in two batches.

Pour batter into prepared dish and cook 15 minutes. Reduce heat to 150°C (300°F), cover with greased aluminium foil and continue to cook 10–15 minutes, until cake is cooked (a skewer inserted in the centre should come out clean). Cool.

To make orange syrup, place sugar and water in a medium saucepan and bring to the boil, making sure the sugar has dissolved. Remove from heat and add orange zest.

Stand for approximately 20 minutes, then add juice to taste. **Note:** The syrup should not be too sweet or too thin. It should maintain a syrupy consistency.

To make Cointreau cream, whip cream and sugar until soft peaks form. Fold in orange zest and Cointreau.

To serve, place a wedge of cake in the centre of each plate. Arrange mango slices over cake and top with a spoonful of cream. Drizzle liberally with orange syrup.

Pear & almond torte with crema di mascarpone

Serves 6

It is always best to grind whole blanched almonds in the food processor as a lot of the oil is already extracted when you buy ground almonds.

2 large or 3 small ripe but firm pears

juice of 1 lemon

80g (3 oz) self raising flour

35g (1 oz) ground almonds

110g (4 oz) caster sugar

pinch salt

4 tablespoons (80ml/3 fl oz) olive oil

160ml (5$\frac{1}{2}$ fl oz) milk

3 eggs

1 teaspoon vanilla essence

few knobs unsalted butter

caster sugar, extra

flaked almonds

sifted icing sugar

Crema di mascarpone

300g (10$\frac{1}{2}$ oz) mascarpone cheese

2 egg yolks

60g (2 oz) icing sugar, sifted

grated zest of 1 lemon

1 vanilla bean, scraped

Preheat oven to 180°C (350°F).

Grease a 22–24cm (8–9 in) rectangular or round earthenware dish.

Leaving skin on, cut pears into wedges and discard core. Toss with lemon juice and set aside.

In a bowl, combine flour, ground almonds, sugar and salt. In a separate bowl, whisk olive oil, milk, eggs and vanilla. Fold into dry ingredients and pour into prepared dish.

Drain juice from pears and discard. Randomly place pears on top of batter. Scatter small knobs of butter and sprinkle with sugar and flaked almonds.

Bake for 30–35 minutes or until the cake springs back to the touch.

To make crema di mascarpone, lightly beat mascarpone with a wooden spoon. Add egg yolks, icing sugar, lemon zest and vanilla scrapings and briefly beat again. If necessary, add a little hot water to correct consistency.

To serve, place a piece of torte on the plate. Dust liberally with icing sugar and serve with a generous spoonful of crema di mascarpone.

Polenta & yoghurt cake with pears in verjuice

Serves 9

Cake

300g (10½ oz) plain yoghurt, preferably Greek-style
100g (3½ oz) polenta
grated zest of 1 orange
grated zest of 1 lemon
120g (4 oz) unsalted butter, softened
220g (8 oz) caster sugar
3 eggs
200g (7 oz) self-raising flour
½ teaspoon bicarbonate of soda
100g (3½ oz) sultanas

Pears in verjuice syrup

juice of 1 orange
juice of 1 lemon
500ml (18 fl oz) verjuice
1 cinnamon stick
1 vanilla pod, split
1 fresh kaffir lime leaf
6 firm pears, peeled and cored

1 cup (250ml/9 fl oz) Greek-style yoghurt
honey

To make cake, preheat oven to 180°C (350°F). Grease a loaf tin and line with non-stick baking (silicone) paper.

Combine yoghurt, polenta and zest. Set aside for 1 hour.

Cream butter and sugar until light and pale. Add eggs one at a time, beating well after each addition.

Sift together flour and bicarbonate of soda. Fold into creamed mixture, then fold in yoghurt mixture. Finally, stir through sultanas.

Pour mixture into prepared loaf tin. Cook for 45 minutes or until a skewer inserted into cake comes out clean. Set aside.

To make syrup, combine all ingredients in a saucepan and bring to the boil. Reduce heat and simmer over low heat for several minutes.

Add pears and cover with a disc of non-stick baking (silicone) paper weighted with a small side plate (to keep pears submerged during cooking). Cook pears until tender but still firm, as they will continue to cook in syrup. Remove from heat and allow to cool in syrup before using.

To serve, place a slice of cake and a poached pear on each plate. Spoon a little syrup over and around cake. Place a spoonful of yoghurt beside cake and drizzle with honey.

Macaroon sandwich, mixed berries & praline cream

Serves 9

Macaroon

300g (10½ oz) ground almonds

500g (1 lb) caster sugar

1 tablespoon (20g) plain flour

1 teaspoon vanilla essence

6 egg whites

½ cup (125g/4½ oz) flaked almonds

1 punnet strawberries

1 punnet blueberries

1 punnet raspberries

2 tablespoons (40ml/1½ fl oz) Cointreau
(orange liqueur)

¼ cup shredded mint leaves

icing sugar

Praline cream

250g (9 oz) caster sugar

water

150g (5 oz) hazelnuts, roasted and skinned

750ml (26½ fl oz) pouring cream (35% butterfat),
whipped

To make macaroons, preheat oven to 180°C (350°F).

Combine dry ingredients in a bowl. Add vanilla and unbeaten egg whites and whisk together.

Rest mixture 5 minutes. Arrange 12 flattened golf ball-sized spoonfuls onto a baking tray lined with non-stick baking (silicone) paper and sprinkle with flaked almonds.

Bake about 20 minutes or until set. Set aside to cool.

To prepare berries, hull and slice strawberries in half. Combine with blueberries and raspberries and gently mix in Cointreau and mint.

To make praline cream, grease a baking tray and set aside.

Place sugar into a saucepan and just cover with water. Heat gently to dissolve sugar completely, then boil rapidly until mixture becomes a dark golden caramel. Do not stir mixture once sugar has dissolved.

Remove caramel from heat immediately and add hazelnuts. Quickly pour mixture over the baking tray and flatten out with a spoon. Leave to set and cool.

When completely cold, break up praline into pieces and crush in a food processor until a medium texture is achieved. Gently fold praline through whipped cream. Set aside.

To serve, place a macaroon on each plate then spoon over a generous portion of praline cream. Distribute berries on cream then top each sandwich with another macaroon. Dust with icing sugar.

*Right: Macaroon sandwich, mixed
berries & praline cream*

Left: Macadamia tart with vanilla cream (recipe page 128)

Right: White chocolate mousse, raspberries & coconut shortbread (recipe page 148)

Left: Frozen bittersweet chocolate parfait with chocolate biscotti (recipe page 122)

Right: Spiced dried fruits, vanilla creamed rice & crisp almond bread (recipe page 147)

Left: Hazelnut & chocolate torte with Frangelico cream (recipe page 124)

Right: Set lemon cream, caramelised peaches & hazelnut crisps (recipe page 145)

Vanilla friands, blueberries & Amaretto cream

Serves 6

Friands are always best on the day. However if they have cooled, friands can be successfully reheated by loosely wrapping them in aluminium foil and warming in a moderate oven.

Amaretto, being an almond liqueur, is not to everyone's taste. You may use Cointreau or your favourite liqueur instead.

170g (6 oz) unsalted butter

200g (7 oz) icing sugar

50g (2 oz) plain flour

130g (4$^{1}/_{2}$ oz) almond meal

6 egg whites

grated zest of 1 lemon

1 teaspoon vanilla essence

1 punnet washed blueberries

icing sugar, extra, for dusting

Amaretto cream

1 cup (250ml/9 fl oz) pouring cream (35% butterfat)

2 tablespoons (40g/1 oz) icing sugar

2 tablespoons (40ml/1$^{1}/_{2}$ fl oz) Amaretto (almond liqueur)

To make friands, preheat oven to 200°C (400°F).

Brush six small metal dariole moulds, approximately 8cm (3 in) diameter x 5$^{1}/_{2}$ cm (2 in) high with melted butter. Dust with flour and shake out excess.

Melt butter and allow to cool to room temperature.

Sift icing sugar and flour together into a bowl. Stir through almond meal.

Beat egg whites to soft peaks. Gently fold into dry ingredients. Add lemon zest and, lastly, fold in cooled melted butter and vanilla.

Fill each dariole mould to three-quarters full. Place on a baking tray and bake 20 minutes, or until friands spring back when touched (similar to sponge texture).

To make Amaretto cream, whip cream with icing sugar until it forms soft peaks. Fold in Amaretto.

To serve, place a warm friand in the centre of each plate. Top with a generous spoonful of Amaretto cream and scatter blueberries over and around. Dust with icing sugar.

Left: Vanilla friands, blueberries & Amaretto cream

Ricotta praline torte with espresso cream

Serves 10

Crust

375g (13 oz) plain flour

3 teaspoons baking powder

150g (5 oz) brown sugar

125g (4¹/₂ oz) almond meal

1 egg, lightly beaten

1 teaspoon vanilla essence

250g (9 oz) unsalted butter, cold

Praline

250g (9 oz) caster sugar

¹/₂ cup (125ml/4¹/₂ fl oz) water

50g (2 oz) pistachios

50g (2 oz) pine nuts

50g (2 oz) almonds

Ricotta filling

800g (1³/₄ lb) ricotta cheese

85g (3oz) praline (above)

30ml (1 fl oz) dark rum (preferably Bundaberg)

60g (2 oz) dark chocolate, shaved

225g (8 oz) caster sugar

Espresso cream

150g (5 oz) caster sugar

6 egg yolks

250ml (9 fl oz) milk

250ml (9 fl oz) pouring cream (35% butterfat)

50g (2 oz) whole coffee beans

2 tablespoons (40g/1 oz) instant espresso coffee dissolved in 3 tablespoons (60ml/2oz) hot water (or 2 short blacks)

300ml (10¹/₂ fl oz) pouring cream (35% butterfat), softly whipped

To make crust, combine all ingredients by hand and bring together to form a crumbly texture. Cover with plastic wrap and chill for 30 minutes.

To make praline, grease a baking tray and set aside.

Combine sugar and water in a small saucepan over low heat and stir until sugar dissolves. Bring to the boil and cook without stirring until syrup becomes a nut brown caramel.

Remove caramel from heat immediately and add all the nuts at once. Quickly pour mixture over the baking tray and flatten out with the back of a spoon. Allow to cool.

When completely cold, break up the praline into pieces and crush in a food processor until a medium texture is achieved.

To make ricotta filling, in a bowl, combine all ingredients together by hand. Set aside.

To make espresso cream, lightly whisk sugar and egg yolks together in a bowl. In a saucepan, bring milk, cream and coffee beans almost to the boil. Whisk into egg mixture. Return to a clean saucepan over moderate heat.

Using a wooden spoon, stir constantly until custard thickens and coats the back of the spoon. Do not let custard boil. Remove from heat and stir in coffee. Refrigerate until cold, then strain. Fold through whipped cream and set aside in the refrigerator.

When ready to assemble, preheat oven to 180°C (350°F). Line the base and sides of a 26cm (10¹/₂ in) springform tin with non-stick baking (silicone) paper.

Press half the crust firmly into the base of the springform tin. Pour in ricotta filling. Crumble remaining crust evenly over top of filling. Cook cake for approximately 1 hour or until a fine skewer inserted in the centre comes out clean.

Serve a slice of ricotta cake with a spoonful of espresso cream.

Set lemon cream, caramelised peaches & hazelnut crisps

Serves 6

Lemon cream

450ml (16 fl oz) pouring cream (35% butterfat)
110g (4 oz) caster sugar
75ml (3 fl oz) lemon juice

hazelnut crisps (Basics page 174)

Caramelised peaches

3/4 cup (6 1/2 oz) caster sugar
water
6 freestone peaches, quartered
60ml (2 fl oz) peach liqueur

To make lemon cream, thoroughly clean 6 bowls, approximately 10–12cm (4–5 in) in diameter x 5–6cm (2–2 1/2 in) high, and place them on a tray.

In a large saucepan, heat cream and add sugar. Stir to dissolve then bring to the boil. Boil for 5 minutes. Remove from heat then pour in lemon juice.

Strain cream through a fine sieve into a jug. Divide between the prepared bowls so that each bowl is approximately half to three-quarters full. Chill until set, preferably overnight.

Prepare hazelnut crisps as recipe directs.

To make caramelised peaches, place sugar in a heavy-based saucepan with enough water to dissolve sugar. Cook over high heat until mixture just begins to turn to a light caramel. Add peach wedges and continue to cook until they begin to soften. During cooking, add more water if necessary to maintain the consistency of the syrup. Remove from heat and gently stir in liqueur.

To serve, place 4 peach wedges on top of each bowl of lemon cream, spooning a little syrup over the top. Serve with hazelnut crisps.

Spiced apple cake with maple caramel

Serves 6

4 Granny Smith apples, peeled, seeded and sliced

juice of 1 lemon

3 cups (375g/13 oz) self-raising flour

2 cups (400g/14 oz) caster sugar

1 teaspoon cinnamon

1 teaspoon mixed spice

1/2 teaspoon nutmeg

pinch of salt

125g (41/2 oz) unsalted butter

3 large eggs

1/2 cup (21/2 fl oz) light olive oil

2 teaspoons (10ml) vanilla essence

Maple caramel

1 cup (250ml/9 oz) Canadian maple syrup

1/2 cup (125ml/41/2 fl oz) pouring cream (35% butterfat)

50g (2 oz) unsalted butter

pinch of salt

vanilla bean ice cream (Basics page 171)

To make cake, grease and line a 20–22cm (8 in) cake tin with non-stick baking (silicone) paper. Preheat oven to 180°C (350°F).

Toss sliced apples with lemon juice and set aside.

Sift flour, sugar, cinnamon, mixed spice, nutmeg and salt together. Rub in butter until mixture resembles breadcrumbs. Whisk together eggs, oil and vanilla. Fold into dry ingredients. Lastly, stir through sliced apples.

Pour batter into prepared cake tin and bake for 40–50 minutes or until cake is cooked when tested with a skewer.

To make maple caramel, combine all ingredients in a small saucepan and bring to the boil. Simmer for 2 minutes, then remove from heat.

To serve, slice warm apple cake into wedges. Place a wedge on the centre of each plate. Place a spoonful of vanilla bean ice cream to one side. Pour warm maple caramel over and around cake.

Spiced dried fruits, vanilla creamed rice & crisp almond bread

Serves 6

This is another dish we used during the Glenfiddich promotional lunch. We matched it with a 12-year-old single malt, again neat, and the combination worked so well, it surprised quite a few people.

300g (10$\frac{1}{2}$ oz) caster sugar

500ml (18 fl oz) water

grated zest of 1 lemon

grated zest of 1 orange

1 cinnamon stick

1 vanilla bean, split and scraped

few slices of fresh ginger

2 kaffir lime leaves

2 star anise

2 earl grey tea bags

400g (14 oz) dried fruit (such as pears, prunes, peaches and apricots)

Vanilla creamed rice

60g (2 oz) unsalted butter

90g (3 oz) caster sugar

125g (4$\frac{1}{2}$ oz) short-grain rice

1 vanilla bean, split lengthwise and scraped

500ml (18 fl oz) milk

500ml (18 fl oz) pouring cream (35% butterfat)

pinch of salt

almond bread (basics page 175)

To make poaching liquid, combine sugar, water, zest, cinnamon, vanilla bean and scrapings, ginger, lime leaves, star anise and tea bags in a large saucepan.

Place over moderate heat and stir until sugar dissolves. Bring to the boil. Reduce heat and simmer for several minutes.

Add dried fruit and continue to simmer until fruit is tender. Remove from heat and allow to cool in liquor. Refrigerate until required.

To make creamed rice, preheat oven to 160°C (325°F).

Melt butter in a heavy-based saucepan over low heat, then add sugar and rice and stir for 5 minutes. Stir in vanilla scrapings, milk, cream and salt and bring to the boil.

Pour mixture into an ovenproof dish approximately 23cm (9 in) x 26cm (10 in) and cover with foil. Place dish into a water bath and bake for 45 minutes–1 hour, stirring every 30 minutes until rice is soft and creamy. The mixture will appear fairly liquid, but the rice will re-absorb this as it cools. Remove dish from oven and stir occasionally while cooling. Refrigerate several hours before serving.

Make almond bread as recipe directs.

To serve, divide fruit between 6 bowls with some of the syrup. Place generous spoonfuls of creamed rice on top and serve with a couple of slices of almond bread.

Note: If the rice has been cooked a day ahead, fold in a little cream prior to serving to soften the mixture.

White chocolate mousse, raspberries & coconut shortbread

Serves 6

When in season, a nice variation to this dish is to serve it with grilled blood plums. For blood plum variation, preheat grill to medium. Halve and remove stones from 6 medium plums. Place plum halves on non-stick oven tray and dust liberally with caster sugar. Grill until plums soften and some colour is achieved.

300ml (10^1/$_2$ fl oz) pouring cream (35% butterfat)

1 vanilla bean, split

200g (7 oz) white chocolate, shaved

3 egg yolks

1 leaf gelatine, soaked in cold water until soft

300ml (10^1/$_2$ fl oz) pouring cream (35% butterfat), whipped to soft peaks

To make mousse, lightly grease six 125ml (4^1/$_2$ fl oz) plastic dariole moulds.

In a saucepan, bring cream to the boil with vanilla bean. Pour into a bowl. Stir in chocolate and whisk in egg yolks. Cook, stirring constantly, over a double boiler until mixture thickens and coats the back of the spoon. Do not boil.

Remove custard from heat and transfer to a bowl. Squeeze out gelatine and discard soaking water. Stir gelatine into custard. Set aside to cool to room temperature.

Gently fold through whipped cream. Pour mixture into prepared moulds and refrigerate overnight.

To make shortbread, grease a 26cm (10^1/$_2$ in) springform tin and line the base with non-stick baking (silicone) paper. Preheat oven to 160°C (325°F).

Cream butter and sugar in a bowl until light and fluffy. Add vanilla and lemon zest. Sift rice flour and plain flour and fold into creamed butter and sugar. Fold in toasted coconut and knead lightly until mixture forms a smooth dough. Do not overwork.

Continued opposite

Coconut shortbread

125g (4½ oz) unsalted butter, softened

80g (3 oz) caster sugar

1 teaspoon vanilla essence

1 teaspoon grated lemon zest

1 tablespoon rice flour

115g (4 oz) plain flour

½ cup (125g/4½ oz) toasted desiccated coconut

1 tablespoon plain desiccated coconut, extra

1 tablespoon caster sugar, extra

1 punnet raspberries, washed

icing sugar, for dusting

Press shortbread into springform tin and mark into 12 wedges. Mix extra coconut and sugar together and sprinkle over shortbread. Bake 25–30 minutes or until a light golden colour. Once cool, carefully cut into wedges with a serrated knife and store in an airtight container.

To serve, run a warm paring knife around the edge of each dariole mould to loosen mousse, then gently squeeze mould so that mousse drops onto the plate (it will be quite soft). Scatter raspberries over and around mousse. Rest a wedge of shortbread, dusted with icing sugar, against mousse.

White chocolate truffle cake with balsamic strawberries

Serves 10

Sponge

250g (9 oz) unsalted butter

250g (9 oz) caster sugar

zest of 1/2 lemon

zest of 1/2 orange

6 eggs, separated

300g (10 1/2 oz) self-raising flour

Crème patissiere

3 egg yolks

60g (2 oz) caster sugar

25g (1 oz) plain flour

250ml (9 fl oz) milk

1 vanilla bean, split

To make sponge, preheat oven to 170°C (340°F). Lightly grease a 26cm (10 1/2 in) springform tin and line with non-stick baking (silicone) paper.

Cream butter and sugar well, add zest, then beat in egg yolks one at a time. Gradually fold in flour.

Whisk egg whites until stiff and fold into mixture in two batches.

Pour mixture into prepared tin. Bake for approximately 40 minutes or until sponge is golden and springs back when touched. Leave sponge to cool in pan.

To make crème patissiere, beat egg yolks and sugar in a bowl until white and creamy, then stir in flour. Scald milk with vanilla bean, then pour a little hot milk onto egg mixture, whisking until smooth. Add remaining hot milk and return to a clean pan. Cook over medium heat, stirring continuously until mixture has thickened and comes to the boil. Beat for a further minute to ensure it is smooth. Strain into a bowl and place plastic wrap directly onto crème patissiere to prevent a skin forming. Chill until required.

Continued opposite

White truffle

400g (14 oz) white couverture chocolate

200g (7 oz) warm crème patissiere (left)

2 leaves gelatine, soaked in water

1 nip Kirsch (cherry liqueur)

2 nips dry sherry

500ml (18 fl oz) pouring cream (35% butterfat), whipped

Balsamic strawberries

3 tablespoons (60g/2 oz) caster sugar

60ml (2 oz) Cointreau (orange liqueur)

1–2 tablespoons (20–40ml/1 fl oz) best-quality balsamic vinegar

1 punnet strawberries, washed, hulled and halved

strawberry jam

hot water

mint sprigs

icing sugar for dusting

To make truffle, gently melt chocolate on medium heat in microwave, or over the top of a double boiler. Combine with crème patissiere then stir in drained gelatine, making sure it is completely dissolved. Add Kirsch and sherry. Cool to room temperature, then fold in whipped cream. Refrigerate until required.

To make balsamic strawberries, 1 hour prior to serving, combine sugar, Cointreau and vinegar to taste. Pour over strawberries.

Remove sponge from tin. Clean, grease and re-line the springform tin with non-stick baking (silicone) paper.

Horizontally slice approximately one-third of the sponge. Return this slice to the springform tin (reserve remaining sponge for another use). Thin strawberry jam with a little hot water and brush onto sponge to moisten. Pour in truffle mix and tap springform tin lightly on bench to remove air bubbles. Refrigerate overnight.

To serve, cut a wedge of cake and place in the centre of a large serving plate. Stir mint sprigs into strawberries and spoon some of the strawberries and syrup on top of cake. Liberally dust with icing sugar.

basics

Savoury shortcrust pastry

300g (10½ oz) plain flour

155g (5½ oz) unsalted butter

salt

1 tablespoon (20ml) very cold water, approximately

Combine flour, butter and salt in a food processor and process until mixture resembles breadcrumbs. Process, adding just enough water to bring pastry together on the blade. Do not overwork. Knead lightly, wrap in plastic food wrap and refrigerate for 1 hour before using.

Sweet shortcrust pastry

350g (12 oz) unsalted butter

155g (5½ oz) icing sugar

4 egg yolks

500g (1 lb) plain flour, sifted

2½ tablespoons (50ml/2 fl oz) very cold water, approximately

In a food processor, cream the butter and sugar together. Add the egg yolks, one at a time, mixing well after each addition. Mix in flour and add just enough water to bring pastry together on the blade. Do not overwork. Knead lightly, wrap in plastic food wrap and refrigerate for 1 hour before using.

To blind bake a pastry tart shell

1 egg, beaten lightly, for egg wash

Preheat oven to 180°C (350°F). Roll out rested pastry 3mm thick and gently ease into tart tin. Rest a further 30 minutes in the refrigerator or freezer. Line pastry shell with a piece of non-stick baking (silicone) paper, parchment or foil and fill with pastry weights such as raw rice or split peas. Bake for 20 minutes. Remove weights and paper and brush egg wash over shell. Reduce oven temperature to160°C (325°F) and bake a further 10 minutes, or until golden.

Clarified butter

250g (9 oz) unsalted butter

Place butter in a small saucepan over low heat, allow it to melt and separate. Carefully pour off melted butter, leaving milk solids behind. Discard milk solids and refrigerate clarified butter.

The main advantage of clarified butter is that it can be heated to a much higher temperature than butter before it burns.

Mayonnaise

Makes 500ml (18 fl oz)

2 egg yolks

2 teaspoons Dijon mustard

2 tablespoons white wine vinegar

juice of half a lemon

250ml (9 fl oz) extra-virgin olive oil

250ml (9 fl oz) olive oil

salt

pinch cayenne pepper

Place egg yolks, mustard, vinegar and lemon juice in a food processor and blend until mixture thickens. Combine oils and, with machine running, slowly drizzle in until the mayonnaise becomes well blended and thick. You may need to thin the mayonnaise with a little hot water.

Transfer mayonnaise to a bowl. Season with salt and cayenne pepper. You may need to adjust acidity with extra lemon juice.

Roasted garlic mayonnaise

Makes 500ml (18 fl oz)

2 egg yolks

2 teaspoons Dijon mustard

2 tablespoons (40ml/1^1/$_2$ fl oz) white wine vinegar

juice of half a lemon

salt/freshly ground black pepper

1 cup (250ml/9 fl oz) extra-virgin olive oil

1 cup (250ml/9 fl oz) vegetable oil

2 heads garlic confit (Basics page 168)

Place egg yolks, mustard, vinegar and lemon juice in a blender. Season well and blend briefly. Combine oils and slowly drizzle into the blender (with the machine running) until the mayonnaise becomes well-blended and thick. Squeeze the flesh from the roasted garlic into the mayonnaise and combine. If the mayonnaise is too think add a little hot water to thin it out. Taste for acidity and seasonings and adjust with lemon juice, salt and pepper.

Chilli tomato chutney / Chilli jam

Makes 500ml (18 fl oz)

2 tablespoons olive oil

1 onion, diced

3 cloves garlic, sliced

1 knob ginger, peeled and grated

3 red chillies, seeds removed and thinly sliced

1 teaspoon brown mustard seeds

1 tablespoon cumin seeds, roasted and ground

2 x 400g (14 oz) cans whole peeled tomatoes

$^1/_4$ cup (60g/2 oz) brown sugar

$^1/_4$ cup (60ml/2 fl oz) Champagne or white wine vinegar

Heat olive oil in a heavy-based saucepan over moderate heat. Sweat onion, garlic, ginger and chillies until onion is transparent. Add mustard seeds and cumin and stir constantly until seeds begin to pop. Stir in tomatoes, sugar and vinegar and bring to the boil. Reduce heat and simmer for 20–30 minutes, stirring often. Set aside to cool.

Chilli oil

Makes 220ml (7$^1/_2$ fl oz)

4 red chillies, seeded and finely diced

2 cloves garlic, crushed

salt/freshly ground black pepper

juice of 2 lemons

$^1/_2$ cup (125ml/4$^1/_2$ fl oz) extra-virgin olive oil

Place chillies, garlic, salt, pepper and lemon juice in a bowl and gradually whisk in the olive oil until well blended. Allow to infuse for several hours.

Beef stock

Makes 4 litres (7 pints)

2¹/₂kg (5 lb) beef neck bones

2¹/₂kg (5 lb) oxtail, cut

2 tablespoons (40ml/1¹/₂ fl oz) olive oil

2 onions, diced

2 carrots, diced

2 sticks celery, diced

2 leeks, washed and sliced

¹/₂ garlic head, halved horizontally

90g (3 oz) field (open-flat or swiss brown) mushrooms, wiped and sliced

¹/₂ cup (125g/4¹/₂ oz) tomato paste

2 cups (500ml/18 fl oz) red wine

1 pig's trotter

1 teaspoon white peppercorns

3 bay leaves

6 sprigs thyme

few parsley stalks

Preheat oven to 220°C (425°F).

Place bones and oxtail in a large roasting pan and roast until well browned. Drain off the rendered fat.

Heat olive oil in a large stockpot over high heat, add onions, carrots, celery, leeks, garlic and mushrooms and sauté until well coloured. Add tomato paste and cook, stirring until liquid reduces by half. Add roasted bones to vegetables with the pig's trotter, peppercorns and herbs and cover well with cold water. Bring to the boil, skimming off any impurities that rise to the surface, then reduce heat and gently simmer for 8 hours. The stock pot may need topping up with water to keep bones submerged. Continue to skim occasionally to remove impurities that will rise to the surface of the pot. Strain stock and refrigerate or freeze until ready to use.

Chicken stock

Makes 3 litres (5 pints)

2kg (4 lb) chicken bones and carcasses

1 carrot, diced

1 onion, diced

1 leek, washed and sliced

1 stick celery, diced

3 cloves garlic, unpeeled, lightly crushed

1 teaspoon white peppercorns

2 bay leaves

4 sprigs thyme

few parsley stalks

Rinse chicken bones in cold water and place in a large stockpot with all remaining ingredients. Cover well with cold water and bring to the boil, skimming off any impurities that rise to the surface. Reduce heat and simmer for 1¹/₂–2 hours or until a good flavour develops. Continue to skim occasionally. Strain stock and refrigerate or freeze until ready to use.

Mushroom stock

Makes about 750ml (1 1/3 pints)

200g (7 oz) button mushrooms
100g (3 1/2 oz) swiss brown mushrooms
1 sprig thyme
2 shallots, finely sliced
2 cloves garlic, thinly sliced
1 bay leaf
1 litre (1 1/2 pints) water

Finely chop mushrooms. Place in a medium sized saucepan with remaining ingredients. Bring to the boil, then simmer for 1 hour. Remove from heat and allow to cool. When liquid is completely cold, strain and refrigerate until required.

Jus

Jus is simply reduced stock or an unthickened meat sauce. Good delicatessens and some restaurants sell jus for the cook's convenience, but otherwise, you can prepare your own, as follows.

4 litres (7 pints) beef stock (Basics page 158, left)

Bring beef stock to the boil over moderate heat. Continue to boil until stock is reduced by two-thirds, occasionally skimming the surface of impurities. The resulting sauce should be thick and glossy.

If, after obtaining the required flavour, the jus is still not of coating consistency, it can be lightly thickened with arrowroot, as follows: Combine 1 tablespoon arrowroot with 1/4 cup (60ml/2 fl oz) cold water, then gradually drizzle just enough into the boiling stock, whisking constantly until the sauce coats the back of a spoon. Strain while hot, cool, then store in small containers in the refrigerator or freezer.

Spicy tomato vinaigrette

Makes 750ml (1¹/₃ pints)

2kg (4 lb) ripe tomatoes, washed well
50ml (2 fl oz) red wine vinegar
pinch cumin seed, roasted, ground
pinch fennel seed, roasted, ground
2 chillies, seeds removed, finely diced
150ml (5 fl oz) extra-virgin olive oil
salt/freshly ground black pepper
dash balsamic vinegar
caster sugar

Chop tomatoes in blender or food processor then pass through a sieve. Pour into a shallow pan and simmer over medium heat until reduced by half. Cool to room temperature.

Transfer reduced tomato mixture to a bowl. Whisk in vinegar, spices and chillies. Drizzle in olive oil, whisking as it is added. Season to taste with salt, pepper and balsamic vinegar. If too acidic, whisk in a little sugar.

Lemon dressing

Makes about 400ml (14 fl oz)

I recommend Hill Farm Mountain Pepper Mustard from Tasmania for this dressing but, if unavailable, any good quality seeded mustard can be used.

100ml (3¹/₂ fl oz) lemon juice
2 teaspoons seeded mustard
1 tablespoon thyme leaves
150ml (5 fl oz) vegetable oil
150ml (5 fl oz) extra-virgin olive oil
salt/freshly ground black pepper

Place lemon juice, mustard and thyme in bowl, whisk in combined oils and season to taste with salt and pepper.

Lime & palm sugar dressing

250ml (9 fl oz) fresh lime juice

250g (9 oz) palm sugar

1 chilli, roughly chopped

few coriander roots, washed

few basil and mint stems, washed

2 fresh Kaffir lime leaves

2 tablespoons roughly chopped ginger

1 stalk lemongrass, bruised

good dash fish sauce to taste

Bring lime juice to the boil in a saucepan. Remove from heat, add palm sugar and stir until it dissolves, returning to heat if necessary. In a mortar and pestle, lightly crush the chilli, herbs, lime leaves, ginger and lemongrass. Add this to the lime juice and palm sugar. Allow to infuse for 1 hour. Set aside to cool and season to taste with fish sauce. Strain before using.

Red wine vinaigrette

Makes 400ml (14 fl oz)

2 cloves garlic, crushed

juice of half a lemon

100ml (3^1/$_2$ fl oz) red wine vinegar

300ml (10^1/$_2$ fl oz) extra-virgin olive oil

salt/freshly ground black pepper

Combine garlic, lemon juice and vinegar in a bowl. Whisk in olive oil and season with salt and pepper to taste.

Burnt orange vinaigrette

Makes 1 cup (250ml/9 fl oz)

600ml (1 pint) orange juice, freshly squeezed
$1/4$ cup (60ml/2 fl oz) extra-virgin olive oil
juice of half a lemon
salt/freshly ground black pepper

Boil the orange juice in a heavy-based saucepan until reduced to 200ml (7 fl oz). Remove from heat and cool slightly before whisking in the olive oil and lemon juice. Season with salt and pepper.

Balsamic dressing

Makes 200ml (7 fl oz)

$1/4$ cup (60ml/2 fl oz) best-quality balsamic vinegar
1 clove garlic, crushed
pinch of caster sugar
salt/freshly ground black pepper
180ml (6 fl oz) extra-virgin olive oil

Place vinegar, garlic, sugar, salt and pepper in a bowl and gradually whisk in the olive oil until well blended.

Slow-cooked duck / Duck confit

Serves 4

4 Maryland (thigh-and-leg) portions from 2.2kg (4$\frac{1}{2}$ lb) ducks

2 sprigs thyme

1 lemon, zest removed in strips

1 orange, zest removed in strips

6 cloves garlic, unpeeled and lightly crushed

3 star anise

salt

500ml (18 fl oz) duck or goose fat or light olive oil, enough to cover legs

Prepare duck portions by removing each thigh bone, then running a sharp knife around the bone just below the knuckle end of each leg – this allows the meat to shrink during cooking. Place portions in a shallow dish and sprinkle with thyme, lemon and orange zest, garlic, star anise and a generous amount of salt. Rub mixture well over portions, then cover and refrigerate for 24 hours.

Preheat oven to 150°C (300°F). Heat fat or oil in saucepan until quite hot, pour over duck then place dish in oven and slow-cook for 2–3 hours or until tender. Cool, then store duck in a clean container covered with cooking fat to seal and preserve it. Refrigerate.

To serve, preheat oven to 180°C (350°F). Remove duck from fat and place in oven until warm, then place under a preheated hot grill just prior to serving to crisp the skin.

Note: It is possible to confit duck legs in light olive oil if duck or goose fat is either difficult to find or you would prefer not to use it. Make sure you use light olive oil, rather than extra-virgin, as its flavour would be overwhelming. However, you cannot achieve the same depth of flavour without using fat.

This duck can be cooked up to 1 week in advance and stored in the refrigerator.

Maryland portions are the thigh-and-leg as one piece, with skin on.

Roasted peppers

peppers (capsicum)
salt/freshly ground black pepper
olive oil

Preheat oven to 250°C (500°F). Wash and dry peppers and rub well with olive oil. Season with salt and freshly ground black pepper. Place peppers on an oven tray and roast until the skin is well-blistered, turning once or twice. You can also roast peppers on a barbecue or under a hot grill. Place peppers in a bowl, cover with plastic food wrap and allow to cool. When the skin has steamed away from the flesh, peel it off and discard with ribs and seeds. Use the roasted flesh as directed in recipes.

Red pepper essence

Makes 1 cup (250ml/9 fl oz)

2 tablespoons (40ml/1¹/₂ fl oz) olive oil
4 red peppers (capsicum), seeded and chopped
4 French shallots, thinly sliced
¹/₄ cup basil leaves
1 star anise
3 cloves garlic, unpeeled and lightly crushed
30ml (1 fl oz) white wine vinegar
200ml (7 fl oz) dry vermouth (preferably Noilly Prat)
600ml (1 pint) chicken stock (Basics page 158)
100ml (3¹/₂ fl oz) orange juice, freshly squeezed
salt/freshly ground black pepper

Heat olive oil in a heavy-based saucepan over moderate heat. Add red peppers, shallots, basil, star anise and whole garlic cloves and gently sweat for 5 minutes or until shallots are softened but not coloured. Add vinegar to pan and cook for 2 minutes. Add vermouth, cook for 2 minutes more, then add stock and bring to the boil. Boil until liquid reduces by half. Remove garlic and star anise, then purée mixture in a blender, adding orange juice. Strain sauce and set aside until required.

This sauce goes well with seafood, grilled polenta and gnocchi.

Rich tomato sauce

Makes 600ml (1 pint)

2 tablespoons (40ml/1¹/₂ fl oz) olive oil

3 French shallots, sliced

4 cloves garlic, finely chopped

2 x 400g (14 oz) cans roma tomatoes, puréed

6 roma tomatoes, skinned and chopped

2 tablespoons herbs such as oregano and thyme, chopped

salt/freshly ground black pepper

pinch of caster sugar, optional

Heat oil in a heavy-based pan over moderate heat and sauté shallots and garlic until shallots are transparent. Add canned and fresh tomatoes and herbs. Reduce heat and simmer for 45 minutes or until tomatoes are well reduced, taking care sauce does not burn. Season with salt and pepper. If sauce tastes too acidic, add a pinch of sugar. For some applications you may need to thin this sauce with a little chicken stock.

Salsa verde

Makes 1 cup (250ml/9 fl oz)

1 cup basil leaves

1 cup flat-leaf parsley

2 cloves garlic, crushed

50g (2 oz) salted capers, well rinsed

3 anchovy fillets in oil, drained, rinsed and dried

1 tablespoon (20ml) red wine vinegar

2¹/₂ tablespoons (50ml/2 fl oz) extra-virgin olive oil

2 teaspoons Dijon mustard

salt/freshly ground black pepper

Finely chop the herbs, garlic, capers and anchovies and place in a bowl. Whisking well, drizzle in the vinegar, then the oil. Flavour with mustard, salt and pepper. Cover and store in the refrigerator.

Champ

Serves 6

1.2kg (2$^1/_2$ lb) pink-skinned, waxy potatoes such as desiree, peeled and diced

250ml (9 fl oz) milk

125ml (4$^1/_2$ fl oz) pouring cream (35% butterfat)

125g (4$^1/_2$ oz) unsalted butter

8 green (spring) onions, thinly sliced diagonally

2 tablespoons salted capers, well rinsed

salt/ground white pepper

Boil potatoes in salted water until tender, drain then pass through a mouli or mash. Place milk, cream and butter in a saucepan, bring to the boil and gradually stir into potatoes to achieve a light, smooth consistency. Fold in onions and capers. Season with salt and white pepper.

Red onion jam

Makes 2 cups (500ml/18 fl oz)

10 red onions, peeled

1 tablespoon (20ml) olive oil

1 tablespoon (20g) unsalted butter

$^1/_4$ cup (60g/2 oz) brown sugar

100ml (3$^1/_2$ fl oz) red wine vinegar

salt/freshly ground black pepper

Halve onions and remove ends. Place flat on a board and cut into thin semi-circles. Heat oil and butter in a wide, shallow heavy-based pan over moderate heat. Add the onions and allow to sweat for 10 minutes. Add vinegar and sugar, and cook for 15–20 minutes or until onions are dark in colour and jam-like in consistency. Season with salt and black pepper. Cool, then store in a covered container in the refrigerator.

Oven-roasted tomatoes

roma tomatoes, halved lengthwise

olive oil

salt/freshly ground black pepper

thyme leaves

balsamic vinegar (optional)

crushed garlic (optional)

Preheat oven to 180°C (350°F). Place tomato halves in a single layer on an greased baking tray. Whisk desired flavourings into a little olive oil and brush liberally over tomatoes. Roast tomatoes for 15 minutes then reduce oven temperature to 120°C (250°F) and roast a further 1^1/$_2$ hours. Tomatoes can be prepared several days in advance and stored in a covered container in the refrigerator until required.

Wet polenta

Serves 6

1 litre (1^3/$_4$ pints) milk

^{1}/$_2$ onion

few sprigs thyme

1 sprig rosemary

2 bay leaves

4 cloves garlic, halved

110g (4 oz) polenta (Glossary)

60g (2 oz) parmesan, freshly grated

1 tablespoon (20g) unsalted butter

salt/freshly ground black pepper

Place milk, onion, herbs and garlic in a saucepan and bring to almost boiling. Place polenta in a large, heavy-based saucepan, strain infused milk onto polenta and whisk until blended. Stir constantly over moderate heat until mixture returns to the boil. Reduce heat to very low and cook, stirring often, for 20–30 minutes or until polenta is cooked and thickened. Fold in parmesan and butter and season with salt and pepper.

Polenta is best served as soon as possible however, if you should need to cook and hold polenta, try this method: Prepare polenta as directed, except omit the parmesan, butter and seasonings. Allow polenta to cool, then cover and refrigerate until needed. To reheat, heat a little extra milk in a saucepan and gradually whisk in the cold wet polenta. Heat through, then stir in cheese, butter and seasonings.

Caponata

Serves 6

3 tablespoons (60ml/2 fl oz) olive oil

1 large eggplant (aubergine), diced

1 large red onion, diced

2 cloves garlic, chopped

2 sticks celery, diced

1 red and 1 yellow pepper (capsicum), seeded and diced

60ml (2 fl oz) red wine vinegar

400g (14 oz) can roma tomatoes, chopped, with juice

2 teaspoons sugar

1/3 cup green and/or black olives, pitted and chopped

1 tablespoon salted capers, well rinsed

salt/freshly ground black pepper

1/4 cup flat-leaf parsley, shredded

Heat oil in a wide, heavy-based saucepan and sauté eggplant until golden. Remove eggplant from pan. Add onion to pan and sauté until golden. Add garlic and cook a further 2 minutes, adding a little more oil if required. Add celery and peppers and cook for 5 minutes.

Deglaze pan with vinegar, then add sugar and tomatoes with their liquid and stir well. Cook uncovered until mixture is fairly dry. Return eggplant to pan with the olives and capers, mix well and season with salt and pepper. Cook a further 5 minutes, then remove from heat and stir through parsley. Serve either warm or cold.

Garlic confit

There are two methods for preparing garlic confit that will give a rich, sweet flavour to the garlic. One is to roast heads of garlic; the other is to simmer them in oil. Squeeze the flesh from the heads of garlic as you require it for recipes.

To roast garlic

Slow-roasted garlic is much more palatable than raw garlic. Preheat oven to 200°C (400°F). Cut off and discard the top one-third from 6 heads of garlic and place, root end down, in the centre of a square of aluminium foil. Drizzle cut tops liberally with extra-virgin olive oil, then wrap heads in foil to enclose completely. Place foil parcel on an oven tray and bake for 1 hour, or until garlic is soft. Cool. Garlic will keep for several days in the refrigerator.

To confit garlic

Cut off and discard the top one-third from 6 heads of garlic and place, root end down, in a saucepan. Cover heads with vegetable oil and cook over low heat for 45–60 minutes or until soft. The long slow cooking is required to develop flavour. Cool, then transfer garlic and oil to a storage container and refrigerate. Use the flesh and flavoured oil as needed in recipes.

Braised oxtail

plain flour, for dusting

8 veal shanks or 2kg (4 lb) cut oxtail

1 onion

1 carrot

1 stick celery

1 leek, halved lengthwise and washed

1/2 cup (125ml/4 1/2 fl oz) olive oil

5 cloves garlic, unpeeled, lightly crushed

few sprigs rosemary

few sprigs thyme

3 tablespoons (60g/2 oz) tomato paste

400ml (14 fl oz) red wine

1–2 litres (1 3/4 – 3 1/2 pints) beef stock (Basics page 158)

Preheat oven to 160°C (325°F).

Season flour with salt and pepper and lightly coat oxtails, shaking to remove the excess. Peel and dice onion, carrot, celery and leek into 1cm (1/2 in) pieces.

Heat olive oil in a heavy-based frying pan and seal oxtails well, transferring them to a large flameproof casserole as they brown. Add the diced vegetables with the garlic and herbs to pan and cook until golden. Add tomato paste and cook for 5 minutes. Spoon mixture over meat in casserole.

Deglaze the pan with wine, stirring to loosen the sediment, and pour mixture into casserole. Add enough stock to casserole to cover contents and bring to the boil. Cover casserole with lid or foil and bake for 2–2 1/2 hours or until meat is tender and pulls away from the bones. Remove from oven and allow to cool in the stock.

Carefully remove all meat from bones, discarding any fat or sinews. Strain the stock, discarding vegetables, and place in a heavy-based saucepan. Boil uncovered, over high heat until reduced to a rich, glossy sauce. Store meat and reduce sauce in separate containers in the refrigerator until needed.

Potato gnocchi

Serves 6 as a starter

750g (1½ lb) bintje potatoes, scrubbed
150g (5 oz) baker's flour (Glossary)
1 egg, lightly beaten
50g (2 oz) parmesan, freshly grated
pinch of nutmeg, freshly grated
salt/freshly ground black pepper

Steam the potatoes until tender, cool a little, then peel and pass through a mouli or sieve. You should have 500g (1 lb) cooked potatoes. Fold flour into potatoes and gently stir in egg, parmesan and nutmeg. Season with salt and pepper. To shape gnocchi, roll mixture into cylindrical shapes 2½cm (1 in) in diameter. Using a floured knife, cut diagonally into 2½cm (1 in) lengths. Do not overwork the mixture or gnocchi will be tough.

Bring a large saucepan of salted water to a simmer. Add gnocchi and cook for 5–8 minutes or until they float – remove one and test. Gnocchi should be cooked in the centre and not gluey. Drain gnocchi, return to pan and coat with prepared sauce.

We have tried a number of potato varieties for gnocchi and find brintje, a waxy potato, works best. Gnocchi can be shaped and cooked in advance. Refresh in iced water, drain then drizzle with a little oil to prevent sticking, and store in the refrigerator until required. Gnocchi will keep 1–2 days.

Cooking chickpeas

Cooking time is dependent on the age of the chickpeas. Fresh dried chickpeas will cook in about 45 minutes.

400g (14 oz) dried chickpeas
1 onion, halved, roots intact
1 bay leaf
few sprigs thyme

Pick over and wash chickpeas, then drain and place in a large bowl. Cover well with cold water and refrigerate overnight. Next day, drain chickpeas, rinse, drain again and place in a large saucepan. Cover well with fresh cold water, add the onion, bay leaf, thyme and bring to the boil, skimming off any impurities that rise to the surface. Reduce heat and simmer until chickpeas are tender, skimming occasionally. Drain, discard flavourings and use as directed in recipes. Will keep 1–2 days, refrigerated.

Vanilla bean ice cream

Makes 1¼ litres (2 pints)

300g (10½ oz) caster sugar

12 egg yolks

2 vanilla pods

500ml (18 fl oz) milk

500ml (18 fl oz) pouring cream (35% butterfat)

In a bowl, lightly whisk sugar and egg yolks together. Split vanilla pods lengthwise and scrape seeds from pods into a 2 litre (3½ pints) saucepan. Add vanilla pods to pan with the milk and cream and bring almost to the boil. Whisk hot milk mixture into eggs then return mixture to clean saucepan over moderate heat. Using a wooden spoon, stir constantly until custard thickens and coats the back of the spoon. Do not let mixture boil. Strain through a fine sieve and refrigerate until cold. Churn in an ice cream machine. Store in freezer.

Toasted coconut ice cream

200g (7oz) caster sugar

12 egg yolks

500ml (18 fl oz) coconut cream

500ml (18 fl oz) pouring cream (35% butterfat)

4 tablespoons desiccated coconut, lightly toasted

Prepare ice cream (above), omitting vanilla. When half churned, add coconut and continue to churn. Store in freezer.

Grand Marnier sorbet

Serves 12

500g (1 lb) caster sugar
500ml (18 fl oz) water
600ml (1 pint) orange juice
1–2 nips Grand Marnier, to taste

In a saucepan bring sugar and water just to the boil, making sure all the sugar has dissolved. Add juice and Grand Marnier. Leave to cool.

When completely cold, churn the mixture in an ice cream machine.

Lemon butter

Makes approximately 500ml (18 fl oz)

4 egg yolks
4 whole eggs
125ml (4$^{1}/_{2}$ fl oz) lemon juice
250g (9 oz) unsalted butter
250g (9 oz) caster sugar

Melt butter in a saucepan. Add to remaining ingredients and mix well. Cook over a double boiler, stirring constantly until mixture thickens and coats the back of the wooden spoon. Do not boil.

Strain into airtight jars and store in the refrigerator.

Orange confit

1 cup (250g/9 oz) caster sugar

1 cup (250ml/9 fl oz) water

1 star anise

1 cinnamon quill

3 whole cloves

1/2 cup (125ml/4 1/2 fl oz) freshly squeezed orange juice

3 oranges, skin and pith removed, thickly sliced

Place sugar, water and spices in a heavy-based pan over moderate heat and cook until mixture is dark caramel, taking care not to let it burn. Remove pan from heat and add orange juice carefully as caramel mixture will spit. Return pan to heat and stir until mixture is smooth. Preheat oven to 160°C (325°F). Place orange slices in an ovenproof dish, pour syrup mixture over and cover with aluminium foil. Bake for 20 minutes or until oranges are soft. Allow oranges to cool in syrup.

Glass biscuits

Serves 6

200g (7 oz) unsalted butter

360g (12 1/2 oz) caster sugar

180g (6 oz) glucose

180g (6 oz) plain flour

In a small saucepan, gently heat butter, sugar and glucose until melted. Pour carefully into a mixing bowl, add flour and bring mixture together, allowing it to cool.

Shape into small balls about the size of a marble and place on a greased baking tray leaving 4–5cm (2 in) between balls.

Cook at 160°C (325°F) for 10 minutes (the mixture will spread like a brandy snap). When the biscuits have cooled, lift them off the tray and store in an airtight container until required.

Hazelnut crisps

100g (3¹/₂ oz) unsalted butter

180g (6 oz) caster sugar

1 teaspoon vanilla essence

90ml (3 fl oz) liquid glucose

90g (3 oz) plain flour, sifted

1 cup (250g/9 oz) hazelnuts, roasted, skinned roughly
chopped and cooled

To make hazelnut crisps, preheat oven to 160°C (325°F). In a small saucepan over very gentle heat, melt butter with sugar, vanilla and glucose, stirring constantly. Transfer to a bowl and add flour and hazelnuts. Stir until mixture comes together. Set aside to cool.

Shape cooled mixture into marble-sized balls, approximately 2cm (³/₄ in) in diameter. Place on a greased baking tray, leaving 4–5cm (2 in) between balls to allow for spreading. Cook for 10 minutes (the mixture will spread like a brandy snap). Cool biscuits on the tray, then lift off and store in an airtight container until required.

Frangipane

250g (9 oz) unsalted butter

250g (9 oz) caster sugar

4 eggs

60g (2 oz) plain flour, sifted

250g (9 oz) almond meal

Preheat oven to 150°C (300°F). Cream butter and sugar together until light and pale. Beat in eggs, one at a time. Combine flour and almond meal and fold through butter mixture. Spoon frangipane into prepared sweet shortcrust pastry shell (Basics page 154) and smooth out top with the back of a hot metal spoon. Bake for 40–50 minutes or until set.

Gingerbread

1¹/₂ cups (375ml/13 fl oz) boiling water

1 cup (250ml/9 fl oz) golden syrup

1 teaspoon bicarbonate of soda

110g (4 oz) unsalted butter, softened

1 cup (9 oz) brown sugar

1 egg

2¹/₂ cups (625g/1¹/₃ lb) plain flour

1 tablespoon baking powder

3 teaspoons ground ginger

pinch ground cloves

1 teaspoon ground cinnamon

pinch nutmeg

¹/₂ teaspoon salt

Preheat oven to 160°C (325°F).

In a saucepan, bring water to the boil. Remove from heat and stir in golden syrup and bicarbonate of soda. Cool slightly.

Cream butter and sugar until light and pale. Add egg and beat well. Stir in golden syrup mixture. Sift together flour, baking powder, ginger, cloves, cinnamon, nutmeg and salt. Fold into creamed butter and sugar.

Pour into a greased loaf pan and bake for 45–50 minutes or until a skewer inserted comes out clean and gingerbread springs back when touched. Leave in pan 5 minutes before turning onto a cake rack.

Almond bread

8 egg whites

240g (8¹/₂ oz) caster sugar

pinch salt

grated zest of 3 lemons

grated zest of 5 oranges

240g (8¹/₂ oz) plain flour

240g (8¹/₂ oz) whole almonds, skin on

Whisk egg whites until stiff peaks form. Gradually add sugar and salt and beat until egg mixture becomes glossy. Gently fold in lemon and orange zest, then fold in plain flour and almonds.

Grease and line a lamington tin, then spoon in mixture. Bake at 160°C (325°F) for approximately 20 minutes or until golden brown.

Allow bread to cool in tin, then turn out onto cutting board. With a serrated knife, thinly slice bread into approximately 2mm slices. Place bread on baking trays in single layers and place in 50°C (100°F) oven for approximately 3 hours or until dry and crisp.

Bread will keep for approximately 1 week. Store in airtight containers.

Sugar syrup

¾ cup (185ml/6½ fl oz) water
½ cup (125g/4½ oz) caster sugar
1 vanilla bean, split

To make sugar syrup, combine water, sugar and vanilla bean in a saucepan. Stir to dissolve sugar. Bring to the boil and simmer for 2 minutes. Remove from heat, cool completely and strain.

Caramel sauce

250g (9 oz) caster sugar
60ml (2 fl oz) water
80ml (3 fl oz) dark rum (preferably Bundaberg)
60ml (2 fl oz) pouring cream (35% butterfat)

Combine sugar and water in a small saucepan and stir over low heat until sugar dissolves. Bring to the boil and boil without stirring until syrup turns a dark caramel colour. Immediately remove from heat and very carefully, as caramel spits, stir in the rum. Return to low heat and stir until smooth, then add the cream and bring to the boil.

Notes for the cook

Equipment

The heavy-based pans referred to throughout this book are sauté pans of heavy gauge mild steel, 22 or 24cm (8^1/$_2$ or 9^1/$_2$ in) in diameter, and about 4cm (1^3/$_4$ in) deep. They are designed to be used both over high flame and in hot ovens. A good brand to look for is Matfer from France. After use, scrub with hot water (no detergent), dry over heat and rub with oil to avoid oxidation.

Using a sauté pan over direct heat, then immediately transferring it to a hot oven is my preferred method of cooking meat. This avoids heat loss and consequently stops the food stewing. These pans are inexpensive and, once you have used this method of cooking meats, you will also be convinced.

However I have described a method of using a domestic frying pan and transferring the food to a hot oven tray if a sauté pan is unavailable.

Our stainless steel cake rings are 24cm (9^1/$_2$ in) in diameter and 4cm (1^3/$_4$ in) high and have no base. A lined springform tin may be substituted for a cake ring although I have yet to find one with low enough sides to suit our tarts.

Standard measures and conversions

1 cup	250 ml (9 fl oz)
1 Australian tablespoon (4 teaspoons)	20 ml
1 UK tablespoon (3 teaspoons)	15 ml
1 teaspoon	5 ml
1 ounce	30 grams
1 fluid ounce	30 ml
1 pint	600 ml (20 fl oz)

Ingredients

checking and adjusting seasonings – refers to tasting a dish and deciding whether or not it requires further flavouring generally with salt or pepper, but could also refer to checking for sweetness or acidity in dressings.

cream – means unthickened cream with at least 35% butterfat, pure cream means unthickened cream with at least 45% butterfat.

egg size – 55–60g free-range are preferred.

herbs – all our recipes use fresh herbs. Prepare by removing wilted or damaged leaves. Wash and spin dry in a salad spinner.

salt – always means good quality sea salt flakes such as Maldon or Fleur de Sel (fine).

salad leaves – Always wash salad leaves in copious amounts of cold water allowing any grit to fall to the bottom. Pick out old, damaged or tough sections/stalks. Place remaining leaves in a salad spinner or clean towel to dry. Dress dry salad leaves in a large kitchen bowl just before serving. This ensures an even coating of dressing.

spices – we always use whole spices and roast and grind them as required. All spices should be purchased and stored whole and separately roasted in a dry frying pan until fragrant. Grind to a powder using a mortar and pestle or coffee grinder.

Glossary

al dente – an Italian term literally translated as 'firm to the bite', used for pasta and risotto, meaning cooked until barely tender, retaining some resistance in the centre.

Asian fried shallots – Asian fried shallots are available in Chinatown or Asian supermarkets.

bain marie – see water bath.

baking (silicone) paper – paper impregnated with silicone to give non-stick surfaces. Widely available at supermarkets.

bakers flour – flour with high gluten content. If unavailable, substitute plain flour adding 10 per cent by weight of gluten flour (available from health food stores).

baking powder – a raising agent consisting of bicarbonate of soda and cream of tartar mixed with a little flour.

balsamic vinegar – a northern Italian specialty vinegar originally from Modena. Vinegar is aged over many years, using a solera system where it darkens and becomes sweet and syrupy. Good balsamic is expensive. Beware of imitation balsamic where caramel is added to a lesser vinegar to enrich it.

bicarbonate of soda – a raising agent which improves the action of baking powder.

blanch – to immerse in boiling, often salted, water for a short period. This action par-cooks and stabilises colour. After blanching, refresh in iced water and drain.

blind bake – Basics page 155.

blini pans – small 12cm (5 in) diameter x 2cm ($^3/_4$ in) high heavy gauge, mild steel pans used for cooking blini, rösti or pancakes. Matfer from France is a good brand to buy. Alternatively, use greased egg rings of similar diameter in a greased heavy-based frying pan.

brioche – a soft, sweet leavened bread enriched with eggs.

butterfly – to debone and flatten gamebird and then open out like the wings of a butterfly.

buttermilk – lightly acidic liquid left after churning butter. It is often used to lighten batters, cakes.

capers – green, unopened flower buds from a Mediterranean shrub. At e'cco we prefer salted capers but ensure they are well rinsed before using.

caramelise – to turn sugar into caramel by gently heating it. Alternatively, caramelising is a technique used to bring out and concentrate the natural sugar of the ingredient (ie. onions, pears, apples, etc), by 'glazing' in a pan with a little oil or butter, to achieve a caramel colour and flavour.

char-grilling – cooking over open flame or in a ridged grill pan.

ciabatta – crusty, flat, rectangular loaf of coarse textured northern Italian bread. Ciabatta literally means slipper.

chillies – the heat of chillies varies greatly with variety and growing conditions. Discarding seeds and membrane will lessen the heat. It is best to taste test raw chillies before using to establish the heat rating.

chorizo – spicy Spanish sausage available fresh or dried. At e'cco we mainly use the fresh variety.

cornflour (cornstarch) – always buy 100 per cent maize flour (not wheaten cornflour).

couverture – good quality chocolate with a high proportion of cocoa butter. It should melt easily on the tongue and not leave a fatty residue on the roof of the mouth. Dark/bitter chocolate has the highest percentage of cocoa butter and lowest percentage of sugar. We recommend and use Valrhona or Callebaut. Avoid compound cooking chocolate.

cream – as in creaming butter and sugar, is the technique of whisking together to dissolve sugar crystals. The mixture will become pale in colour and aerated.

crème fraîche – a distinctly sharp, semi-sour cream. Can be substituted with sour cream.

dariole mould – round, flat-bottomed, metal cup with flared sides, 125ml ($4^1/_2$ fl oz) capacity.

deglaze – the action of adding stock, wine or water to a hot pan after browning ingredients. This incorporates any solids remaining in the pan into the liquid which is then added to the dish, giving added flavour.

devein – to remove intestinal tract from prawns, firstly remove the shell. Using a saté stick or skewer, insert it under the intestinal tract and gently lift to remove.

dice – to chop into small, even cubes.

double boiler (double saucepan) – a method of gentle cooking by indirect heat obtained by sitting a tight-fitting saucepan or heatproof bowl over another pan quarter-filled with gently simmering water.

duck fat – available canned from delicatessens and gourmet food stores.

fold – to gently incorporate ingredients with a lifting and cutting action to avoid loss of aeration.

frisèe – a fine, frizzy-leafed vegetable also known as curly endive. While it resembles a lettuce it has a sharp and slightly bitter flavour.

gelatine – half a teaspoon of gelatine powder equals one gelatine leaf. Leaf gelatine is considered superior to powder as it will set clear rather than cloudy.

goat's cheese – freshly made goat's cheese (goat ricotta or curd) in its simplest form, is mild and soft. As it ages and loses moisture if becomes stronger in flavour and more densely textured. Goat's cheese can be aged coated in ash, vine leaves, straw or it can form its own rind. These different outer layers will influence the flavour.

Granny Smith apple – firm, juicy, tart green-skinned cooking apple.

hokkien noodles – thick, wheat-based egg noodles available vacuum-packed in supermarkets or fresh in Asian food stores.

icing sugar (confectioner's sugar) – powdered pure version of white granulated sugar. Icing mixture has added cornflour to prevent lumps.

julienne – to cut into matchstick-sized strips.

jus – unthickened sauce or gravy, reduced from stock.

kaffir lime leaf – whole leaf added to dishes for its lime flavour, available fresh or frozen. Mainly used in southeast Asian cookery, especially Thai.

kibbled pepper – coarse ground pepper.

mandoline – stainless steel manual slicing utensil.

mascarpone – sweet, rich cream (70–75% butterfat), usually made from cow's milk.

mouli – a mill used to purée fruit, soup or vegetables.

mustard fruits – Italian glacé fruits packed in spicy mustard syrup.

olive oil – 'extra-virgin' refers to first quality olive oil with low acidity. Flavour varies regionally and between olive varieties from golden coloured, very mild oils to peppery, dark green. Price is a good guide to quality but choose a flavour you enjoy. Use sparingly in dressings, over breads and where the flavour of the oil is paramount. When not marked 'extra-virgin', olive oil is from a subsequent or heavier pressing of the olives. This type of oil is used for cooking and frying. It is generally a lot less expensive than extra-virgin olive oil.

palm sugar – Asian style sugar produced from palm sap, available as dark brown or light golden in colour. We prefer to use light palm sugar.

pancetta – salted pork belly. Closely related to bacon.

parmesan – best quality is Parmigiano Reggiano from the Emilia-Romagna region of Italy. Genuine wheels have Parmigiano Reggiano stamped on the rind. This high quality parmesan is mainly used for garnishing and eating. A lesser quality grana padano or hard-grating cheese is generally used for cooking.

peanut oil – ground nut oil.

pickled ginger – generally thinly sliced ginger, pickled in brine or rice vinegar, pinkish in colour. Available at most supermarkets and Asian food stores.

pin boning – to remove bones from salmon fillet with tweezers or pliers.

poach – gentle method of cooking in barely simmering liquid.

polenta – cornmeal.

porcini – Italian name meaning "little pig" for meaty type of mushroom originating in Tuscany. It is the same variety as the French cep and is available dried.

praline – caramel combined with nuts then ground into a fine or coarse powder. While almonds have traditionally been used for praline, other nuts such as hazelnuts can also be used.

prosciutto – salted, air-dried Italian style ham, always sliced paper thin.

purée – to pass through mouli or sieve, so no solids remain.

ramekins – refers to a ceramic pot used in baking. Available in various sizes but more commonly recognised as a small soufflé dish, 8–10cm (3–4 in) diameter.

refresh – to quickly chill vegetables or salad leaves by plunging into iced water.

risotto rice – Arborio, Carnaroli or Vialone Nano are all excellent Italian risotto rice varieties. We prefer Vialone Nano. Risotto rice has the ability to cook to a creamy consistency with the grains remaining separate with a firm centre.

roasting nuts – nuts are best roasted by placing in a cake tin in a 180°C (350°F) oven until golden. Different varieties roast at different times.

roasting or grilling bacon, pancetta, prosciutto – Preheat oven to 190°C (375°F). Lay sliced meat in a single layer on greased or baking (silicone) paper-lined oven tray and roast in oven until crisp. Meat may also be grilled until crisp.

ruby chard – young red stemmed variety of silverbeet, also known as rainbow chard or red swiss chard.

salmon pearls – salmon roe (eggs).

sauté – to toss in small amount of fat (butter or oil) over high heat.

sauternes – A small wine region in Bordeaux in France. Wines from this region produce grapes affected by Botrytis, a mould which causes ripe grapes to shrivel and produce a very concentrated juice. The term generally refers to sweet dessert wines.

scoring – to make shallow incisions on the skin or outer layer of an ingredient to aid cooking.

seal – to quickly cook food (usually meat) on both sides over very high heat, to seal in juices.

sear – to very quickly cook over fierce heat.

shallot (French shallot) – also known as eschalot or golden shallot. Small, elongated golden brown/pink-skinned onions which grow in tightly formed clusters like garlic. They have a fine, delicate slightly sweet and nutty flavour.

simmer – heated to just below boiling point where the surface of liquid should ripple but the bubbles should not break the surface.

sourdough – a chewy bread made using a fermented starter giving its characteristic sour taste. Sourness varies depending on recipe used.

springform tin – a circular metal cake tin with removable base that is held together by an expanding clamp on the side. Available in various diameters generally 6cm (2½ in) high.

star anise – aniseed flavoured, eight-pointed pod of an evergreen Asian tree. Buy whole then roast and grind as required.

sweat – to cook gently over moderate heat, no colour should be developed.

tahini – Middle Eastern sesame seed paste, refrigerate after opening or it will oxidise.

terrine – 1.2 litre (2 pints) capacity, 25cm (10 in) length x 7cm (2¾ in) height lidded dish, generally of cast iron, we recommend Le Creuset.

tomato paste (concentrated purée) – good quality Italian brands offer better flavour than supermarket varieties.

truffle oil – extra-virgin olive oil infused with the flavour of truffles. We prefer Terrabianca brand.

vanilla essence – always use good (Bourbon) quality vanilla essence, not imitation essence. Whole pods should be preferably Grade A1 from Madagascar, pliable and coated in vanillan crystals.

verjuice – the juice extracted from large unripened grapes, which imparts a subtle tartness and acidity to vinaigrettes and sauces. Verjuice must be refrigerated once opened.

vinegars – always buy good quality vinegars. The wine vinegars used at e'cco are the Spanish brand, Forum, varietal vinegars. Both their Chardonnay (white) and Cabernet Sauvignon (red) are excellent.

water bath (bain marie) – a method of baking delicate foods using a cloth-lined dish filled with enough hot water to come halfway up the sides of the vessel containing the food.

wine – never cook with wine that you wouldn't consider drinking.

witlof – a small compact vegetable from the endive family, also known as Belgian endive, available all year round. The most common variety is white with pale green tips; a red variety is also available. An extremely versatile ingredient, it resembles a lettuce but is more sharply flavoured.

zest/zesting – outer layer of citrus fruit, without any white flesh (pith). Most often used finely grated. The utensil for removing zest is known as a zester but a stiff-bladed vegetable peeler can be used.

Index

Page numbers in **bold** refer to photographs